pillows

Handcrafted

Handcrafted pillows

Sew and Embellish Pillows in the Decorator Looks You Love

Linda Neubauer
Joanne Wawra

Creative Publishing
international
Chanhassen, Minnesota

Copyright © 2005
Creative Publishing international
18705 Lake Drive East
Chanhassen, Minnesota 55317
1-800-328-3895
www.creativepub.com
All rights reserved

Creative Publishing
international

President/CEO: Ken Fund
Vice President/Publisher: Linda Ball
Vice President/Retail Sales: Kevin Haas

HANDCRAFTED PILLOWS

Executive Editor: Alison Brown Cerier
Managing Editor: Yen Le
Senior Editor: Linda Neubauer
Project and Photo Stylist: Joanne Wawra
Photographer: Tate Carlson
Photo Direction and Cover Design: Lois Stanfield
Page Design: Kari Johnston
Illustrator: M. Deborah Pierce
Production Manager: Stasia Dorn
Samplemakers: Arlene Dohrman, Sheila Duffy, Teresa Henn

Contributors: Fairfield Processing Corporation.

Photo credit pages 100 and 111: "Three Fillies," by Lois Stanfield. Copyright ©
2005 by Lois Stanfield. All right reserved. Equestrian equipment and apparel were
donated by Equestrian Paradise, Long Island, Minnesota.

Library of Congress Cataloging-in-Publication Data

Neubauer, Linda.
        Handcrafted pillows : sew and embellish pillows in the decorator
        looks you love / by Linda Neubauer and Joanne Wawra.
        p. cm.
        Includes index.
        ISBN 1-58923-151-1 (soft cover)
1. Pillows. 2. Fancy work. I. Wawra, Joanne. II. Title.
TT410 .N48 2005
746.9–dc22
                                                2004021212

Printed in Shenzhen, China:
10 9 8 7 6 5 4 3 2 1

Contents

Pillow Talk

Strolling through an upscale home interior store on our lunch hour one day, we noticed how the lavish designer pillows gave each room setting a boost into the realm of extravagant décor. They were made with fabulous fabrics and embellishments and often had three-digit price tags. Being longtime sewers and crafters, we automatically (and uncontrollably) critiqued each pillow on how it was made, what could have been done better, and of course, how much was invested in materials. After all, neither of us would ever dream of spending that much on a pillow when pillows are just about the easiest thing in the world to make. Soon our casual browsing turned into a mission to seek out each and every pillow, feign shock at the price, and then analyze how we could do better.

But why stop there? For more than ten years at Creative Publishing international, we have researched, experimented with, and taught every sewing, crafting, and needle art technique around. It only seemed natural that we should turn our little game into an idea for a new book. Pillows truly are very easy to make, and we can show you step-by-step how it's done.

Begin with the first section, where you will learn construction steps for the five basic pillow styles. You'll find several alternatives for closures and decorative edge finishes, and learn about the options for filling your pillows. The handcrafted pillows in the sections that follow build on those basics; each features a special fabric or technique that gives it unique style.

In pillow making, you have choices—lots and lots of choices. Almost any fabric can be used, though many of our pillows were designed with a particular type in mind. The selection of trims and embellishments is nearly endless. Many techniques used in the pillows were borrowed from other areas of crafting, such as quilting, beading, painting, stamping, rug hooking, embroidery, and even foiling. There's something here for every taste and decorating style. Most projects require basic sewing skills, nothing too complicated.

We invite you to copy our designs or improvise with individual touches to suit your décor. Enjoy choosing fabrics and trims, experimenting with new techniques, and creating your own handcrafted pillows.

ABOUT THE AUTHORS

Linda Neubauer is the senior editor for the lifestyles books of Creative Publishing international. She has written and edited dozens of books on sewing, quilting, and crafting. She lives in Minneapolis.

Joanne Wawra is the project and photography stylist for the sewing, crafting, and other lifestyles books of Creative Publishing international. She lives in Minneapolis.

HOW TO *Sew* A PILLOW

The purpose of this first section is to teach the fundamental techniques for making pillows in five basic styles with various options for closures and decorative edges. With this information and your choice of fabrics and trims, you could make hundreds of unique pillows. You will also refer to these basics as you work on the designer pillows in the other four sections.

THE FIVE STYLES STEP-BY-STEP

Pillows come in several basic styles: knife-edge, mock box, flange, box, and bolster. From these styles, you can design countless pillows in a wide range of fabrics, using decorative techniques and embellishments to suit every décor, mood, and budget. Each of the pillow projects in this book is designed around one of these basic styles.

The instructions for each style described in this section are for a pillow cover that is stitched closed. If you think you'll never need to remove the stuffing to clean the pillow cover, this is a suitable finish. For pillow covers that are removable, see the section on closures (pages 24 to 27). Each project in this book includes closure suggestions; it's up to you to decide what's best for your particular projects.

Pillow covers can be made to fit ready-made square, rectangular, and round pillow forms (page 36). If you want the pillow to be plump and firm, plan the finished size to be at least 1" (2.5 cm) smaller than the pillow form size. If you prefer that your pillow be softer and less plump, plan the finished size to be the same as the form. For pillows in nonstandard sizes and shapes, you can make forms to fit and fill them with the loose stuffing of your choice. For pillows without removable inserts, stuff the filling directly into the pillow cover.

Knife-edge Pillows

The term "knife-edge" means that the front and back of the pillow are the same size and shape and are joined by a single seam around the perimeter. If desired, that seam can also incorporate a decorative element, such as welting, fringe, or a ruffle. Knife-edge pillows can be square, rectangular, or almost any shape you wish to create, though some shapes are better suited to this style than others. Round knife-edge pillows, for instance, will pucker unattractively around the edge.

Square and rectangular knife-edge pillows tend to develop "dog ears" when they are stuffed, because they are thicker in the center than around the edges. This effect can be prevented with the simple shaping technique described in steps 2 to 4, opposite.

HOW TO MAKE A KNIFE-EDGE PILLOW

1 Determine the desired finished size of your pillow and add 1" (2.5 cm) in both directions for seam allowances. Cut the pillow front and back along the fabric grainlines.

2 Fold the front into fourths. Mark a point halfway between the corner and the fold on each open side. At the corner, mark a point ½" (1.3 cm) from each edge.

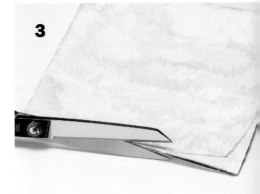

3 Trim a gradually tapering sliver of fabric from the marked point on the fabric edge to the marked corner point. Repeat on the adjoining side to shape the corner.

Tip: *Cut through all four layers at once, if the fabric is fairly lightweight. For heavier fabrics, trim both sides of one corner and then use it as a pattern to trim the remaining three corners.*

4 Unfold the front and use it as a pattern for trimming the back.

5 Pin the pillow front to the back, right sides together. Stitch ½" (1.3 cm) seam, pivoting at the corners. Leave an opening on one lengthwise-grain side for stuffing the pillow.

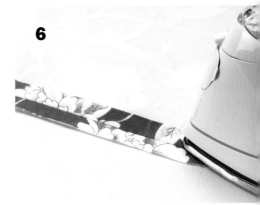

Tip: *If you will be inserting a pillow form, leave an opening about two-thirds the length of the side. For loose stuffing, a smaller opening will do.*

6 Press the seams flat. Then turn back the upper seam allowance and press with the tip of the iron in the crease of the seam. In the area of the opening, press both seam allowances back.

7 Turn the pillow cover right side out. Square up the corners, using a point turner or similar pointed utensil inserted through the opening. Press lightly.

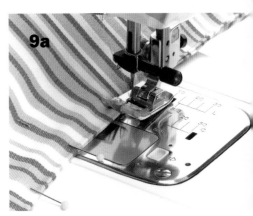

8 Compress and insert the pillow form, making sure the form sits squarely inside the cover; add fiberfill in the corners, if necessary. Or stuff the pillow with the desired stuffing.

9a Pin the opening closed, aligning the pressed folds. Edgestitch by machine.

9b Pin the opening closed, aligning the pressed folds. Slipstitch the opening closed by hand.

Mock Box Pillows

The mock box pillow, a variation of the knife-edge style, is cube-shaped with soft, undefined edges. Unlike the knife-edge pillow that tapers in depth toward the outer edges, the mock box pillow is chunkier with a consistent depth from center to sides. The depth is created by stitching a vertical seam in each corner of the pillow cover, which shortens the length and width. The length of that seam determines the pillow depth. The larger the pillow, the deeper it can be. For instance, a large floor pillow looks well proportioned with a depth of 6" (15 cm), whereas a smaller sofa pillow looks better at a depth of 2½" to 3" (6.5 to 7.5 cm). The perimeter seam circles the pillow halfway between the front and back. If desired, this seam can incorporate welting.

   The chart opposite shows the cut sizes needed for the finished sizes of mock box pillows that will fit standard pillow forms. Cut sizes include ½" (1.3 cm) seam allowances.

HOW TO MAKE A MOCK BOX PILLOW

1 Cut out the pillow front and back, aligning the sides to the fabric grainlines. Refer to the chart below for cut size guidelines.

2 Pin the pillow front to the back, right sides together. Stitch ¹/₂" (1.3 cm) seam, pivoting at the corners. Leave an opening on one lengthwise-grain side for stuffing the pillow. Press the seam allowances open.

Tip: *It is helpful to insert a sleeve roll or firm cardboard tube into the pillow cover for pressing the seam allowances open.*

3 Pull the front and back away from each other at one corner, and refold the fabric so that a new corner is formed with the seams in the center. Pin through the seams from front to back to ensure they are aligned.

4 Measure along the seam and mark a point a distance from the corner that equals half the desired pillow depth. Draw a line through the point, perpendicular to the seam, from fold to fold. The length of the line equals the total desired pillow depth. Stitch on the marked line. Do not trim off the corner triangle.

5 Repeat steps 3 and 4 at each corner. Repeat for the corners of the pillow form, if desired. Turn the pillow cover right side out. Insert the form and close the opening as in steps 7 to 9 on page 11.

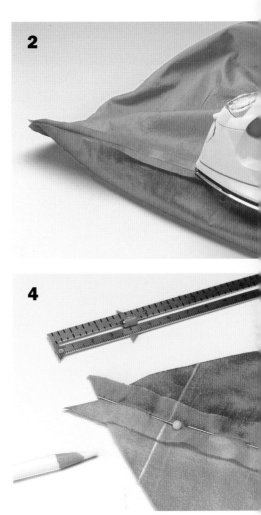

Finished Size	Depth	Cut Size	Form Size
10" × 10" (25.5 × 25.5 cm)	2" (5 cm)	13" × 13" (33 × 33 cm)	12" × 12" (30.5 × 30.5 cm)
11½" × 11½" (29.3 × 29.3 cm)	2½" (6.5 cm)	15" × 15" (38 × 38 cm)	14" × 14" (35.5 × 35.5 cm)
13" × 13" (33 × 33 cm)	3" (7.5 cm)	17" × 17" (43 × 43 cm)	16" × 16" (40.5 × 40.5 cm)
14½" × 14½" (36.8 × 36.8 cm)	3½" (9 cm)	19" × 19" (48.5 × 48.5 cm)	18" × 18" (46 × 46 cm)
16" × 16" (40.5 × 40.5 cm)	4" (10 cm)	21" × 21" (53.5 × 53.5 cm)	20" × 20" (51 × 51 cm)
19" × 19" (48.5 × 48.5 cm)	5" (12.7 cm)	25" × 25" (63.5 × 63.5 cm)	24" × 24" (61 × 61 cm)
24" × 24" (61 × 61 cm)	6" (15 cm)	31" × 31" (78.5 × 78.5 cm)	30" × 30" (76 × 76 cm)

Flange Pillows

A flange is flat fabric that extends beyond the stuffed portion of a pillow. There are several ways to make a flange. A single flange is formed from two layers of fabric seamed together around the edge. For a double flange pillow, each flange is self-lined. Raw-edge flange pillows are made from two layers of reversible fabrics that do not ravel, such as polar fleece, felt, faux suede, real suede, or leather. Individual self-lined flange strips can be sewn into the seams of a knife-edge pillow to make a pillow with contrasting flanges that are interrupted at the corners.

The flange width can vary to suit your pillow's size and design. A good width for sofa pillows is 1½" to 2½" (3.8 to 6.5 cm); larger pillows can have wider flanges. Unless the fabric is quite stiff, however, wide flanges tend to flop forward, so that is something to consider if you want to display the pillow standing upright.

The easiest way to make a flange pillow is to stitch the opening closed by machine. However, if you want to be able to remove the pillow form, plan for a plain or decorative overlap closure, a centered zipper closure on the back, or an invisible zipper closure between double flanges.

HOW TO MAKE A SINGLE FLANGE PILLOW

1 Determine the finished size of the stuffed area of the pillow plus twice the width of the flange. Add 1" (2.5 cm) to the width and length for ½" (1.3 cm) seam allowances all around. Cut out the pillow front and back, aligning sides to the fabric grainlines.

2 Follow steps 5 to 7 for the knife-edge pillow (page 11). Mark the depth of the flange from the seamed outer edge. Pin the layers together along the marked line to keep them from shifting. Stitch on the marked line, leaving an opening of the same size parallel to the outer opening. (photo)

3 Insert the pillow form or stuffing into the inner area; do not stuff the flange.

4 Topstitch the inner area closed, using a zipper foot. Slipstitch the flange closed, or edgestitch around the entire flange. (photo)

HOW TO MAKE A RAW-EDGE FLANGE PILLOW

1 Determine the finished size of the stuffed area of the pillow plus twice the width of the flange. Cut out the pillow front and back, aligning sides to the fabric grainlines, if necessary.

2 Mark the depth of the flange on the pillow front. Pin the front to the back, wrong sides together, along the marked line to keep them from shifting. Stitch on the marked line, leaving an opening along one side for inserting the pillow form.

3 Insert the pillow form or stuffing into the inner area. Topstitch the inner area closed, using a zipper foot.

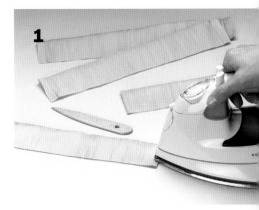

HOW TO MAKE A PILLOW WITH CONTRASTING FLANGES

1 Follow steps 1 to 4 for a knife-edge pillow (page 11). Cut four flange strips the same lengths as the pillow sides and 1" (2.5 cm) wider than twice the desired width of the flange. Fold each strip in half lengthwise, and stitch ½" (1.3 cm) seams across the ends. Turn right side out and press. (photo)

2 Pin the flange strips to the outer edges of the pillow front, ½" (1.3 cm) from the corners, aligning the raw edges. Baste a scant ½" (1.3 cm) from the edges. (photo)

3 Follow steps 5 to 9 for the knife-edge pillow (page 11) to complete. Take care that the finished ends of the flanges do not get caught in the stitching.

Box Pillows

Box pillows are cube-shaped, having fronts and backs of the same shape and size joined together with a strip of fabric known as a boxing strip. Using this technique, you can make a pillow in any shape, including circles, rectangles, hexagons, triangles, hearts, and stars. Standard pillow forms can be used for square box pillows, but to fill the pillow depth more consistently, make the pillow cover with a width and length 2" (5 cm) smaller than the pillow form size. For nonstandard shapes and sizes, make your own pillow form or insert loose stuffing directly into the pillow cover.

HOW TO MAKE A RECTANGULAR BOX PILLOW

1 Determine the finished width, length, and depth of the pillow. Add 1" (2.5 cm) to the width and length for ½" (1.3 cm) seam allowances all around. Cut out the pillow front and back, aligning sides to the fabric grainlines. Cut the boxing strip, with the length equal to the finished distance around the pillow plus 1" (2.5 cm) for seam allowances and the width equal to the finished pillow depth plus 1" (2.5 cm) for seam allowances. If the boxing strip will need to be pieced, allow 1" (2.5 cm) for each piecing seam.

2 Piece the boxing strip together, if necessary, using ½" (1.3 cm) seam allowances. Stitch the short ends of the strip, right sides together, to form a continuous loop. Mark both long edges of the boxing strip with the lengths of each side of the pillow, using a ⅜" (1 cm) clip into the seam allowances. Do not use a joining seam as one of the marks.

3 Pin the boxing strip to the pillow front, right sides together, raw edges even, matching the clip marks on the boxing strip to the pillow corners.

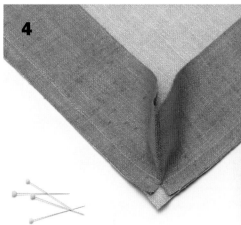

4 Stitch ½" (1.3 cm) seam. At each corner, stop with the needle down in the fabric, and pivot the fabric. The clip marks will spread, allowing the fabric to turn the corner.

5 Pin the other side of the boxing strip to the pillow back, right sides together, matching the clip marks to the corners. Stitch the seam as in step 4, leaving an opening for stuffing the pillow.

6 Press the seams flat. Then, on each seam, turn back the upper seam allowance and press with the tip of the iron in the crease of the seam. In the area of the opening, press both seam allowances back.

7 Turn the pillow cover right side out. Square up the corners, using a point turner or similar pointed utensil inserted through the opening. Press lightly.

8 Compress and insert the pillow form, making sure the form sits squarely inside the cover; add fiberfill in the corners, if necessary. Or stuff the pillow with the desired stuffing. Slipstitch the opening closed.

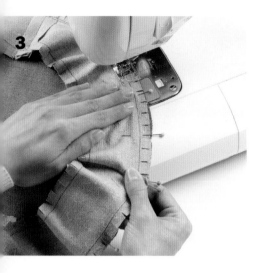

HOW TO MAKE A ROUND BOX PILLOW

1 Make a pattern for the pillow front and back, using a string-and-pencil compass. Add 1/2" (1.3 cm) seam allowance all around. Cut out the pattern; use it to cut out the pillow front and back. Multiply the finished diameter by 3.14, and round the measurement to the nearest fraction of an inch (millimeter) to determine the finished length of the boxing strip; add 1" (2.5 cm) for seam allowances. Cut the boxing strip the desired finished width plus 1" (2.5 cm) for seam allowances.

2 Stitch the boxing strip into a continuous loop, as in step 2 for the rectangular box pillow. Stitch a scant 1/2" (1.3 cm) from each edge of the boxing strip. Then clip the seam allowance every 1/2" (1.3 cm) up to, but not through, the stitching line.

3 Pin-mark the pillow front, pillow back, and boxing strip into fourths. Pin the boxing strip to the pillow front, right sides together, raw edges even, matching the pin marks. With the boxing strip facing up, stitch 1/2" (1.3 cm) seam.

Tip: *The clips allow the boxing strip to fan out and fit the pillow front edge evenly. Keep the raw edges of the boxing strip aligned to the outer edge of the pillow front, and stitch just to the left of the first row of stitching, so that the first row will be hidden inside the pillow cover.*

4 Stitch the other side of the boxing strip to the pillow back, leaving an opening for turning and stuffing. Finish the pillow as in steps 6 to 8 for the rectangular box pillow, disregarding the reference to corners.

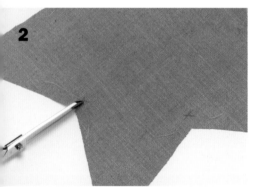

HOW TO MAKE A BOX PILLOW WITH INSIDE CORNERS

1 Make a pattern for the pillow front and back, adding 1/2" (1.3 cm) for seam allowances all around. Measure the entire outer seamline and add 1" (2.5 cm) to determine the cut length of the boxing strip. Cut the boxing strip to the desired width plus 1" (2.5 cm); piece together as necessary.

2 Mark the seamlines at any inner corners of the pillow front and back. Using short straight stitches, staystitch on the seamline, about 1" (2.5 cm) each side of the inner corners, pivoting at the corners. Clip up to, but not through, the stitching lines at the corners.

3 Prepare the boxing strip as in step 2 for the round box pillow, above, in areas where the boxing strip will follow an outer curve. Pin the boxing strip to the pillow front, right sides together. Stitch with the boxing strip facing up in areas of straight lines or outer curves. Stop stitching within 2" (5 cm) of any inner corners, and resume stitching 2" (5 cm) beyond the corner.

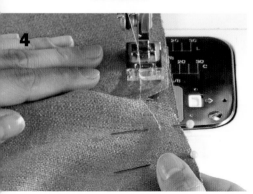

4 Complete the stitching at the inner corners with the boxing strip on the underside. Stitch just to the inside of the staystitching lines.

5 Attach the other side of the boxing strip to the pillow back, leaving an opening for turning and stuffing. Finish the pillow.

Bolster Pillows

Bolsters are cylindrical pillows that offer support for the neck or lower back. With their interesting shape, they are a great addition to the "pillow scene" and versatile enough to be used on beds, sofas, chairs, and window seats. In its simplest form, a bolster is merely a rectangle sewn into a cylinder and drawn closed at each end with a drawstring in a casing. An alternative is to make the cylinder extra long and tie the ends with decorative cording so the pillow resembles a wrapped candy. In a tailored version, the bolster ends are capped with circles of fabric. The cylinder itself can be pieced together from two or more fabrics and the seams can be embellished with welting or other decorator trims.

Bolster forms are available in several sizes, or you can make your own, following step 1, page 20, for a simple bolster.

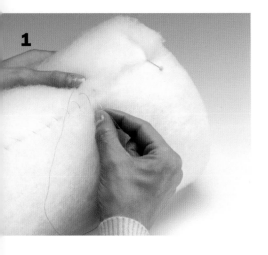

HOW TO MAKE A SIMPLE BOLSTER

1 Cut a rectangle of batting about 1 yd. (0.92 m) long, with the width equal to the desired finished length of the bolster. Roll the batting with the desired firmness (the looser you roll it, the softer the bolster will be) until it is the desired diameter; cut off any excess. Whipstitch the cut end to the roll.

2 Cut a rectangle of fabric with the width equal to the circumference of the bolster form plus 1" (2.5 cm) and the length equal to the length of the bolster form plus the diameter plus 1½" (3.8 cm) for casings.

3 Press under ¼" (6 mm), then ½" (1.3 cm) on each short end of the fabric to form the casings. Unfold the ends. Fold the fabric in half lengthwise, right sides together. Stitch ½" (1.3 cm) seam on the lengthwise edge, beginning and ending with backstitches ¾" (2 cm) from the ends; press the seam open.

4 Refold the casings. Edgestitch along the inner folds; reinforce the stitches at the openings. Turn the bolster cover right side out.

5 Thread narrow cording into the casings. Insert the bolster form. Draw up the cording and tie securely. Tuck the cord ends inside the opening, if desired.

Tip: *If the bolster form is not completely covered at the ends, place pieces of matching fabric over the ends before tying the cords. The tightness of the drawstring will keep them in place.*

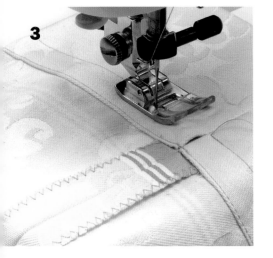

HOW TO MAKE A CANDY WRAPPER BOLSTER

1 Make a bolster form as in step 1 for a simple bolster, if necessary. Cut a rectangle of fabric with the width equal to the circumference of the bolster form plus 1" (2.5 cm) and the length equal to the length of the bolster form plus three times the diameter.

2 Press under ¼" (6 mm) on each short end; unfold. Fold the fabric in half lengthwise, right sides together. Stitch a ½" (1.3 cm) seam on the lengthwise edge, beginning and ending with backstitches ¾" (2 cm) from the ends; press the seam open.

3 Refold the ¼" (6 mm) at the open ends. Then fold the ends under half the diameter of the bolster. Edgestitch along the inner folds; reinforce the stitches at the openings. Stitch again ½" (1.3 cm) from the fold, forming a casing.

4 Thread narrow cording into the casings. Turn the bolster cover right side out. Insert the bolster form. Draw up the cording and tie securely. Tuck the cord ends inside the opening. Tie decorative cording around the gathers at each end, if desired.

HOW TO MAKE A TAILORED BOLSTER

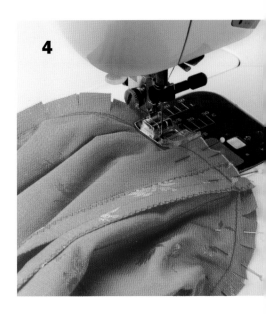

1 Make a bolster form as in step 1 for a simple bolster, if necessary. Cut a rectangle of fabric with the width equal to the circumference of the bolster form plus 1" (2.5 cm) and the length equal to the length of the bolster form plus 1" (2.5 cm). Cut two circles of fabric for the ends with the diameter equal to the diameter of the bolster form plus 1" (2.5 cm).

2 Fold the rectangle in half lengthwise, right sides together. Stitch a ½" (1.3 cm) seam on the lengthwise edge, leaving an opening for turning and inserting the bolster form; press the seam open.

3 Stitch a scant ½" (1.3 cm) from the outer edge of each end of the cylinder. Clip into the fabric every ½" (1.3 cm) up to, but not through, the stitching line.

4 Pin a circle to one end, right sides together, aligning the raw edges. The cylinder ends will fan out at the clips. Stitch a ½" (1.3 cm) seam, keeping the outer edges even. You should be stitching just inside the first stitching line. Repeat at the opposite end.

5 Turn the bolster cover right side out. Insert the bolster form. Slipstitch the opening closed.

CLOSURE OPTIONS

Pillows that are used for comfort, tossed about, and handled a lot need closures that will allow you to easily remove the stuffing so the covers can be laundered or dry cleaned occasionally. The options include conventional zippers, invisible zippers, and lapped closures.

The pillow style influences the closure choice as well as the closure location. Invisible zippers, for instance, work well in the seams of plain knife-edge pillows or mock box pillows, especially when the pillows are decorative on both sides. If a knife-edge pillow has welting or ruffles, though, it can be more difficult to insert a zipper in the seam. A conventional zipper or lapped closure in the pillow back would be easier in such cases. If a box pillow needs a zippered closure, it is usually applied into a section of the boxing strip so that the pillow is reversible. Flange pillows that require removable covers can have zippered, lapped, hook and loop tape, or buttoned closures in the back or decorative buttoned closures in the front.

Sometimes the closure itself is the main decorative feature of the pillow. Items borrowed from the fashion world—like fancy buttons, toggles, frogs, buckles, and fabric or ribbon ties—give these home décor pieces a couture touch.

$\mathscr{Z}$ippers

Conventional polyester zippers (not the separating kind) can be inserted in a seam between pieces of the pillow back. The seam can be centered in the pillow back or placed close to one edge so that it is less visible; the seam allowances hide the zipper teeth. Invisible zippers, which must be installed with the use of a special presser foot, are usually placed in the seam between the pillow front and back, where they almost disappear.

Make the zipper closure long enough so that removing and inserting the pillow form will not strain the zipper ends. As a general rule, use a zipper that is at least three-fourths the pillow width. Zippers can be shortened, if necessary.

HOW TO SHORTEN A ZIPPER

1 Close the zipper. Mark the desired length on the zipper tape. Drop or cover the sewing machine feed dogs; attach a button or appliqué presser foot, if you have one. Set the machine to the widest zigzag setting, and stitch in place across the zipper teeth for several stitches at the mark.

2 Cut off the excess zipper 1/2" (1.3 cm) below the stitches. (photo)

HOW TO INSERT A CONVENTIONAL ZIPPER

1 Cut the pillow back 1" (2.5 cm) wider than the front to allow for 1/2" (1.3 cm) seam allowances at the closure. Fold the pillow back in half, right sides together, if you want the closure to be centered in the pillow back. Fold one edge in 1³/4" (4.5 cm), if you want the closure near one edge. Press.

2 Mark the fold at the location of the zipper stops. Stitch 1/2" (1.3 cm) from the fold, from the pillow edge to the first mark; backstitch. Machine-baste to the second mark. Shorten the stitch length again and backstitch; then stitch to the opposite edge. Cut on the fold; press the seam allowances open. (photo)

3 Center the closed zipper facedown over the seam, with the stops at the marks. Glue-baste or pin to the seam allowances only. Finish the seam allowances, catching the zipper tape in the stitches. (photo)

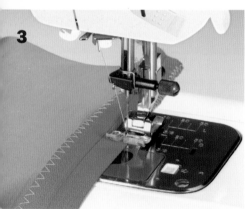

4 Spread the pillow back flat, right side up. Mark the top and bottom of the zipper coil with pins. Center a strip of 1/2" (1.3 cm) transparent tape over the seam from pin to pin. Topstitch a narrow rectangle along the edges of the tape, using a zipper foot. Stitch slowly as you cross the zipper teeth just beyond the stops. Remove the tape. Pull threads to the underside and knot. Remove the basting stitches. (photo)

5 Finish the pillow, following the general directions for the pillow style. Rather than leave an opening for turning, simply open the zipper before stitching the final seam.

HOW TO MAKE A ZIPPER CLOSURE IN A BOXING STRIP

1 Purchase a zipper that is about 2" (5 cm) shorter than one side of a square box pillow or one-third the circumference of a round pillow. Cut a boxing strip for the zipper section 2" (5 cm) wider than the desired finished width of the boxing strip and equal in length to the zipper tape. Cut a boxing strip for the remaining pillow circumference 1" (2.5 cm) wider than the desired finished width and about 6" (15 cm) longer than the remaining circumference.

2 Press the boxing/zipper strip in half lengthwise, right sides together. Machine-baste 1/2" (1.3 cm) from the fold. Cut on the fold; press the seam allowances open.

3 Center the closed zipper facedown over the seam. Glue-baste or pin to the seam allowances only. Finish the seam allowances, catching the zipper tape in the stitches.

4 Turn the zipper strip faceup. Center a strip of 1/2" (1.3 cm) transparent tape over the entire seam. Topstitch along the edges of the tape from end to end, using a zipper foot (no need to cross the zipper). Remove the tape. Remove the basting stitches.

5 Press under 2" (5 cm) on one short end of the boxing strip. Lap the fold over the upper end of the zipper strip to cover the tab. Stitch through all the layers 1 1/2" (3.8 cm) from the fold. (photo)

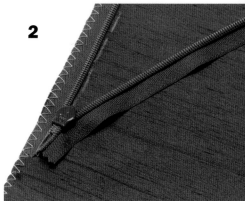

6 Trim the boxing/zipper strip to the finished pillow circumference plus 1" (2.5 cm) for seam allowances. Pin the cut end to the bottom of the zipper strip, right sides together. Stitch 1/2" (1.3 cm) seam, stitching slowly over the zipper teeth. Press the seam allowances away from the zipper. Finish the pillow, following the general directions on page 17. Rather than leave an opening for turning, simply open the zipper before stitching the final seam.

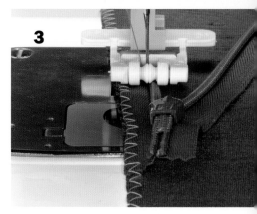

HOW TO INSERT AN INVISIBLE ZIPPER

1 Open the zipper; press open the zipper tape from the wrong side to unroll the coils. Center the zipper along one long edge of the pillow back. Mark the right side of the pillow back at the ends of the zipper coil; transfer the marks to the pillow front. Mark the 1/2" (1.3 cm) seamline on the fabric, using removable fabric marker or chalk.

2 Position the open zipper on the pillow back, right sides together, with the zipper coil aligned to the seamline and ends of coil aligned to the marks. Glue-baste or pin in place. Finish the seam allowance, catching the zipper tape in the stitches. (photo)

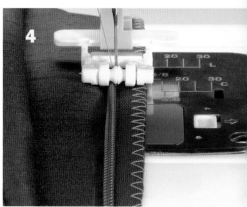

3 Attach the invisible zipper foot to the machine; position the top of the zipper coil under the appropriate groove of the foot. Slide the zipper foot on the adapter to adjust the needle position so stitching will be very close to the coil; on heavier fabrics set the needle position slightly away from the coil. Stitch, starting at the top of the zipper, until the zipper foot touches the pull tab at the bottom. (photo)

4 Secure the other side of the zipper to the pillow front, as in step 2. Position the coils under the zipper foot; slide the zipper foot on the adapter to the opposite side, and adjust the needle position. The bulk of the fabric will be on the opposite side of the needle. Stitch until the zipper foot touches the tab. (photo)

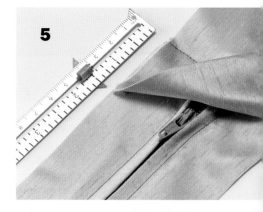

5 Close the zipper; pin the pillow front and back right sides together above and below the zipper. Adjust the zipper foot to get as close as possible to the zipper. Stitch the rest of the seam.

6 Open the zipper. Attach the general purpose presser foot, and finish the pillow, following the general directions for the pillow style. Rather than leave an opening for turning, simply open the zipper before stitching the final seam.

$\mathscr{L}$apped $\mathscr{C}$losures

A lapped closure is simply two hemmed edges that overlap, similar to that on a button-down shirt. The edges can be held together with fasteners, such as hook and loop tape, snap tape, or buttons. If the edges are overlapped slightly deeper, fasteners are not necessary. Closure that are strictly functional can be placed in the center of the pillow back or near one side. On the other hand, decorative closures showing off fancy buttons or toggles can be positioned on the pillow front.

HOW TO SEW A PLAIN LAPPED CLOSURE

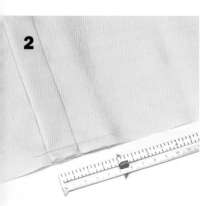

1 Cut two pieces for the pillow back with the length equal to the finished pillow length plus 1" (2.5 cm) and the width equal to half the finished pillow width plus 3½" (9 cm). Press a 1" (2.5 cm) double-fold hem in one long edge of each back piece. Stitch along the inner fold of each piece.

2 Overlap the hemmed edges 2" (5 cm), right sides up. The inner folds will align. Baste across the hem ends. Follow the general pillow directions to complete the pillow. Rather than leave an opening for turning, turn the pillow right side out through the overlapped hems.

HOW TO SEW A HOOK AND LOOP TAPE LAPPED CLOSURE

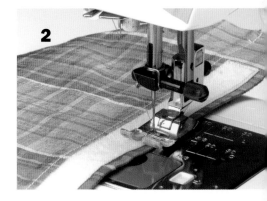

1 Cut two pieces for the pillow back with the length equal to the finished pillow length plus 1" (2.5 cm) and the width equal to half the finished pillow width plus 3" (7.5 cm). Press a 1" (2.5 cm) double-fold hem in one long edge of each back piece. Stitch along the inner fold of one piece.

2 Cut strips of ³⁄₄" (2 cm) hook and loop tape 3" (7.5 cm) shorter than the hemmed side. Center the loop side of the tape on the right side of the stitched hem. Stitch around the outer edges of the tape.

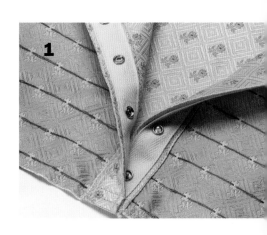

3 Unfold the hem edge of the other pillow back piece. Center the hook side of the tape on the right side of the fabric, between the two pressed folds; stitch around the outer edges of the tape. Refold the hem, and stitch.

4 Overlap the hems and seal the tape. Baste across the hem ends. Follow the general pillow directions to complete the pillow. Rather than leave an opening for turning, unseal the tapes to turn the pillow right side out.

HOW TO SEW A BUTTONED CLOSURE

1 Follow step 1 for the hook and loop closure, but stitch both hems in place. Stitch the desired number of evenly spaced buttonholes parallel to and down the center of the hem of one pillow back piece (or front piece, if closure is decorative). Overlap the hems and mark the button placement through the center of each buttonhole onto the underlapped hem. Sew on the buttons.

2 Overlap and button the hems. Baste across the hem ends. Finish the pillow, following the general directions for the pillow style. Rather than leave an opening for turning, unbutton the hems to turn the pillow right side out.

HOW TO SEW A SNAP TAPE LAPPED CLOSURE

1 Follow the directions for the hook and loop tape closure, above, but extend the snap tape sides into the seam allowances at the ends of the opening. Be sure the snaps align before stitching.

DECORATIVE EDGES

The seams around a pillow are the perfect place for decorative accents. While defining the pillow's lines, accents like fabric-covered welting and twisted cord welting also lend stability and give the pillow a tailored, classic look. Ruffles soften the pillow lines and create a casual, romantic appearance. Fringes, in every style imaginable, boost plain pillows into the designer category.

Welting

Cording, available in several sizes, can be covered with fabric to make welting. Choose a cording diameter that will complement the pillow's size and shape and work well with the pillow fabric. Narrower welting is more tailored and well suited to small pillows made with lightweight fabrics. Thicker welting is more casual and more prominent in the overall design of the pillow. In order to round corners and fit curves smoothly, fabric strips for making welting are cut on the bias.

Twisted cord welting is an ornate alternative to fabric-covered welting, and is available in a wide range of styles, colors, and sizes. A welt tape, or lip, is attached to a decorative cord for sewing into a seam. From the right side of the welting, the inner edge of the lip is not visible. For easier stitching and a neat appearance on the pillow front, the welting is applied to the pillow back first, right side up. The ends of the welting can be twisted together to join them inconspicuously.

Decorative trims, including twisted welting, tend to unravel easily. Before cutting these trims in the fabric store, the clerk should wrap the trim with tape and cut through the center of the taped area. Likewise, when you begin a project, wrap the trim with tape before cutting to a workable length. Before making final cuts, saturate the trim with liquid fray preventer or fabric glue and allow it to dry completely, then cut through the center of the sealed area.

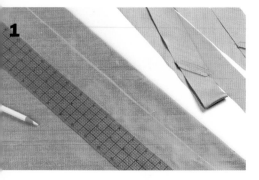

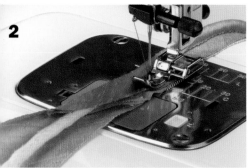

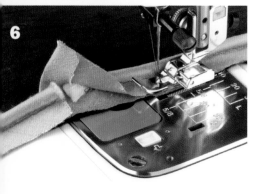

HOW TO MAKE FABRIC-COVERED WELTING

1 Fold the fabric diagonally, aligning the cut end to the selvage. Cut bias strips parallel to the fold 1" (2.5 cm) wider than the cording circumference. Piece strips together to a length a few inches (centimeters) longer than the distance to be welted.

2 Fold the fabric strip around the cording, right side out, aligning the raw edges. Using a cording foot or zipper foot, machine-baste close to the cording. Keep the cording straight and smooth as you sew.

3 Stitch the welting to the right side of the pillow aligning the raw edges and starting 2" (5 cm) from the end of the welting. Clip and ease the welting at corners; ease the welting around curves.

4 Stop stitching 2" (5 cm) from the point where the ends will meet. Cut off one end of the welting so it overlaps the other end by 1" (2.5 cm).

5 Remove the stitching from one end of the welting, and trim the ends of the cording so they just meet.

6 Fold under ½" (1.3 cm) of fabric on the overlapping end of the welting. Lap it around the other end; finish stitching the welting to the pillow edge.

7 Finish the pillow, following the general directions for the style. On seams that carry welting, use a cording foot or zipper foot. With the wrong side of the welted piece facing up, stitch inside the previous stitching line, crowding the stitches against the welting.

HOW TO ATTACH TWISTED CORD WELTING

Tip: *When you attach twisted welting to a square or rectangular pillow, be sure to taper the pillow corners as in steps 2 and 3 on page 11.*

1 Pin the twisted welting to the pillow back, right sides up, with the beginning and end along one side (not at a corner). Mark each corner with a pin. Remove the trim.

2 Hand-tack the lip to the cord ¼" (6 mm) from each side of each pin. Cut away ½" (1.3 cm) of lip at each corner mark. This will make it easier to attach the welting as is rounds the corners.

3 Stitch the twisted welting to the pillow back, right sides up, using a zipper foot; align the edge of the welt lip to the raw edge of the fabric. Round the cord at the corners and stitch only on the fabric. Leave 1½" (3.8 cm) unstitched between ends; leave 3" (7.5 cm) tails.

4 Loosen the cord from the lip in the area of the join. Trim the lip ends so they overlap 1" (2.5 cm). Separate the cord plies; wrap the end of each ply with tape. Arrange the plies so those on the right turn up and those on the left turn down.

5 Insert the plies on the right under the crossed lip ends, twisting and pulling them down until the welting is returned to its original shape. Secure in place using tape.

6 Twist and pull the plies on the left over the plies on the right until the twisted ends look like continuous twisted welting from both sides. Tape in place.

7 Position the zipper foot on the left of the needle, if possible. Place the pillow back to the right of the needle; this will allow you to stitch in the direction of the cord twists, rather than against them. Machine-baste through all layers to secure the welting. If you are unable to adjust your machine to stitch in this position, remove the presser foot and stitch manually over the thick cords. Be sure the presser foot lever is down so the thread tension is engaged.

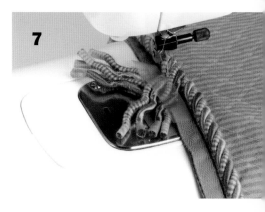

8 Finish the pillow, following the general directions for the style. On seams that carry twisted welting, use a zipper foot. With the wrong side of the welted piece facing up, stitch inside the previous stitching line, crowding the stitches against the welting.

Ruffles

Because they will be visible from both sides, self-lined ruffles are best for pillows. Taper square pillow corners, as in steps 2 and 3 on page 11, before attaching ruffles. Then round the corners rather than pivot sharply. The finished pillow will appear square and the ruffles will lie more smoothly around the corners.

HOW TO MAKE RUFFLES

1 Cut strips of fabric for the ruffles on the lengthwise or crosswise grain of the fabric twice the desired finished width plus 1" (2.5 cm). Piece enough strips together to reach a length two to three times the pillow circumference; piece the strips together in diagonal seams to reduce bulk.

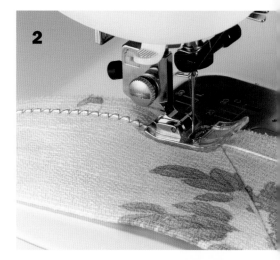

2 Stitch the ends of the ruffle strip together in a diagonal seam, forming a circle. Fold the strip in half lengthwise, right sides together. Press the fold, if desired, or leave it unpressed for softer ruffles. Prepare the raw edges for gathering by zigzagging over a cord, such as crochet cotton or dental floss, within the 1/2" (1.3 cm) seam allowance.

3 Fold the ruffle into fourths. Make a 3/8" (1 cm) clip into the seam allowances at each fold. Arrange the ruffle on the right side of the pillow front, with the zigzagged cord on top and raw edges even. For a square pillow, match the clips to the corners of the pillow front; for a rectangular pillow, match the clips to the centers of the sides; for a round pillow, match the clips to quarter-marks along the outer edge. Pin at the marks.

4 Pull up the gathering cord until the ruffle fits the areas between the marks. Distribute the fullness evenly, allowing extra fullness at the corners so the ruffle can fan out. Pin the ruffle in place. Secure the gathering cord by wrapping the ends around pins.

5 Machine-baste the ruffle to the pillow front, stitching just inside the gathering row.

6 Finish the pillow, following the general directions for the style. On seams that have ruffles, with the wrong side of the ruffled piece facing up, stitch just inside the previous stitching line.

Fringe

Decorator fringes are available in a wide range of styles and colors, many with coordinating braids or tassels. They may be made from synthetic or natural fibers or a combination of fibers with interesting textural effects. Some fringes have decorative headings and are meant to be sewn on the outer surface of the pillow. Others have plain headings that should be sewn into a seam, encasing the heading and exposing only the fringe.

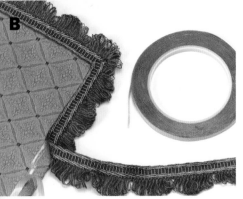

HOW TO ATTACH FRINGES

Fringe without decorative heading (A). Taper the corners on square-corner pillows. Machine-baste the fringe to the right side of the pillow front, placing the heading within the 1/2" (1.3 cm) seam allowance and the fringe facing inward. At the ends, cut the fringe between the loops and hand-stitch the cut ends to prevent raveling; butt the ends together. Finish the pillow following the general directions for the style.

Fringe with decorative heading (B). Before stuffing the pillow, pin the fringe around the front outer edge of the finished pillow cover, aligning the inner edge of the heading to the outer edge of the pillow. Miter the heading at corners. If the heading is thick or textured, use paper-backed, two-sided fabric adhesive. Secure a thin, flat heading using fabric glue or paper-backed fusible adhesive strips.

Brush fringe (A) is a dense row of yarns, all cut to the same length. When you see it in the store, the cut edge is usually secured with a chain stitch, which should be left intact until you have finished the pillow. The stitches are then easily removed and the brush fringe can be fluffed out by steaming and gently rubbing.

Cut fringe has a decorative heading and is similar to brush fringe, but is usually not as dense. The cut yarns of this fringe are often multicolored in a blend of fibers. The decorative heading can be sewn or glued to the pillow, perhaps over a seam or along an edge, and the fringe is allowed to hang free.

Loop fringe (B) is made with either a decorative or plain heading and is available in a variety of fibers. Just as the name implies, the fringe is composed of a series of overlapping looped yarns, cords, or ribbons. The loops may be all the same length or arranged in a pattern of varying lengths.

Tassel fringe (C) is a continuous row of miniature tassels attached to a decorative heading. The tassels are often separated by loops and may be multicolored and multifibered.

Ball fringe (D) is a continuous row of pompoms hanging from a plain heading. Though recognized as a casual craft fringe, some styles of ball fringe are more ornate and suitable for embellishing pillows.

Bullion fringe (E) is a continuous row of twisted cords attached to a plain or decorative heading. Styles range from very heavy, long fringe to lightweight, short fringe with single-color or multicolor cords. Cotton bullion fringe is casual, while rayon or acetate bullion fringes can be used for elegant pillows.

Beaded fringes (F) are very chic. They are available in many styles; some resemble cut, loop, or ball fiber fringes but are made with hundreds of beads in all sorts of shapes, sizes, and colors. Bead fringes with decorative headings or ribbons can be sewn to the outer surface of a pillow; those with a plain heading are caught in outer seams where the beads can dangle and swish.

Feather fringe (G) is a trendy embellishment for pillows that are meant to be more decorative than useful. The feathers are usually secured to a plain tape that can be concealed inside a seam or covered with another trim.

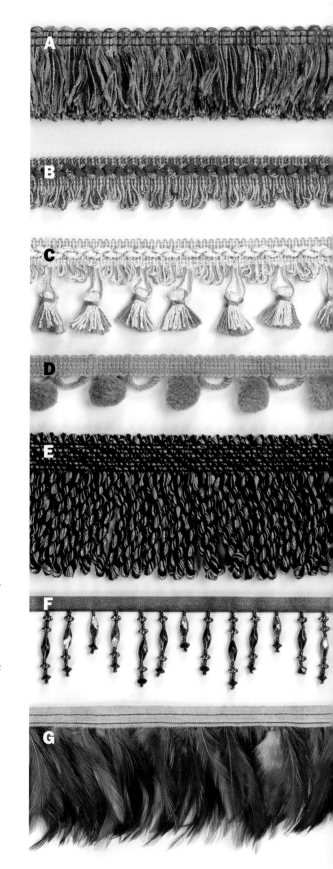

FORMS AND FILLINGS

Pillows get their shape from natural or synthetic fillings. Depending on the shape, size, and purpose of a pillow, you can fill it with loose filling or with a pillow form. Forms are great for pillows that will be laundered or dry cleaned because they are easily inserted and removed through a zippered or lapped closure. If you want to be able to remove the filling for cleaning a pillow that is a nonstandard size or shape, make a muslin-covered form in the same shape as the pillow and fill it with the desired material. Loose filling can be stuffed directly into the pillow cover if you intend to stitch it closed. This is the best option for pillows like the Soothing Eye Bag (page 140), filled with flaxseed, and the Hot or Cold Shoulder Wrap (page 144), filled with rice.

Forms are available in knife-edge squares from 10" to 30" (25.5 to 76 cm), rectangles, rounds, and bolsters. The most expensive forms are filled with down or a mix of down and feathers. Down-filled pillows can be shaped and slouched to conform to the corner of a sofa. They mold comfortably to your body when you lean on them, but they are brought back to billowy plumpness with a little fluffing. Polyester fiberfill forms imitate some features of down, but they are more resilient or springy than down. Fiberfill forms are lower in cost, washable, and nonallergenic. Different brands of fiberfill forms

vary in quality and price—some are more plump, guaranteed not to separate or clump, and have fabric covers as opposed to thin nonwoven synthetic covers.

Manufactured forms aren't necessarily ready for use, especially if they seem high through the center with filling that doesn't reach the corners. You can open a seam and adjust the filling, if necessary, filling out the corners and creating a more even thickness. If you want more plumpness, add some loose fiberfill before sewing the form closed. To use a knife-edge form for a box or mock box pillow, move filling out of the corners and follow steps 3 and 4 for the Mock Box Pillow, page 13, stitching from the outside of the form.

BOLD & CREATIVE

Pillows can be a canvas for crafting, giving you a chance to try new techniques or showcase your skill. The pillows in this section are an invitation to get creative! The designs will draw attention with bold colors or intriguing surface textures. Each of these pillows could become the focal point of a room, setting the particular mood or adding a punch of color.

Quilted and Beaded

Quilting gives a surface depth and texture. For the silk plaid fabric used in this pillow, quilting also shows off its natural rich sheen. What could be easier than using the lines of the plaid as a quilting guide? (Similarly, you could quilt along the lines between stripes or quilt the outlines of flowers and leaves on a floral print.) To further accent the puffy grid created by the quilting stitches, a sequin and teardrop bead are sewn in the center of each square. Colorful beads will catch the light and draw attention to the pillow.

MATERIALS

Basic sewing supplies

1/2 yd. (0.5 m) plaid silk fabric

1/2 yd. (0.5 m) low-loft batting

1/2 yd. (0.5 m) muslin or other lightweight cotton fabric

Quilter's safety pins

Thread to match or blend with fabric

Walking foot, optional

Sequins and teardrop beads in colors to match the fabric

Hand needle small enough to go through beads

Invisible zipper

16" (40.5 cm) square pillow form

CLOSURE SUGGESTION

Invisible zipper in bottom seam

Quilted and Beaded

1 Cut two 18" (46 cm) squares for the pillow front and back. If you are using a plaid or stripe, make sure the pieces will match at the seams. Cut two 18" (46 cm) squares of batting and two 18" (46 cm) squares of muslin.

2 Sandwich a square of batting between the pillow front and the muslin, with the right side of the pillow front facing up. Plan the placement of the quilting lines. Pin the layers together using quilter's safety pins spaced about 4" (10 cm) apart. Avoid placing pins where you will be stitching. Repeat for the back.

2

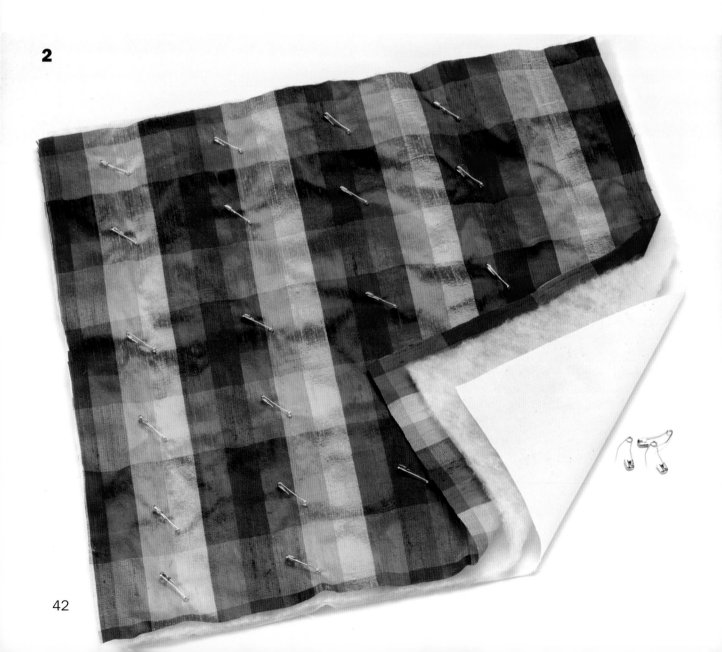

3 Attach a walking foot to the sewing machine. Using a straight stitch about 2 mm long, stitch a line near the center across the pillow front in both directions to anchor the batting. Then stitch the remaining quilting lines between bars in the plaid. Repeat for the pillow back.

4 Remove the safety pins. Trim the front and back to 17" (43 cm), centering the plaid. Hand-stitch a sequin and bead to the center of each quilted square.

5 Attach an invisible zipper (page 25) to the bottom seam between the pillow front and back, taking care to match the plaid. Stitch the remaining seams, following the directions for a knife-edge pillow (page 10). Turn right side out and insert the pillow form.

$\mathscr{I}$ridescent $\mathscr{O}$verlays

$\mathscr{I}$ridescent sheers are available in a range of brilliant hues. They have a mesmerizing moiré effect as light catches them from different angles. Here, iridescent sheers are used as flanged overlays for simple knife-edge pillows. Pintucks stitched with a twin needle add a tailored touch to the overlays. Satin or cotton sateen fabric in a solid color seen in the sheer is used for the inner knife-edge pillow. To avoid unsightly closures in the sheer fabric, both the inner pillow and the overlay are stitched closed.

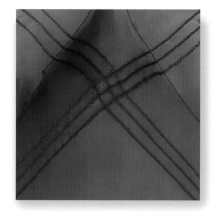

MATERIALS

Basic sewing supplies

1/2 yd. (0.5 m) satin or cotton sateen fabric for inner pillow

14" (35.5 cm) square knife-edge pillow form

5/8 yd. (0.6 m) iridescent sheer

Thread to match a color apparent in the sheer fabric

Twin needle, size 2.8/80

Pintuck presser foot

Zipper foot

$\mathcal{I}$ridescent $\mathcal{O}$verlays

1 Make a 14" (35.5 cm) square knife-edge pillow (page 10). Set aside.

2 Cut a front and back for the overlay 19½" (49.8 cm) square. Mark a line on the overlay front 4½" (11.5 cm) from each edge, using chalk or disappearing fabric marker.

Tip: *It is important to begin with pieces that have been cut perfectly on-grain. Pull a thread along each cutting line for accuracy.*

3 Stitch on the marked lines using the twin needle and a pintuck presser foot. Stitch two more rows on each side, each ¼" (6 mm) closer to the edge, using the pintuck foot as a guide. Grooves on the bottom of the pintuck foot ride over previous ridges, keeping the stitching lines parallel.

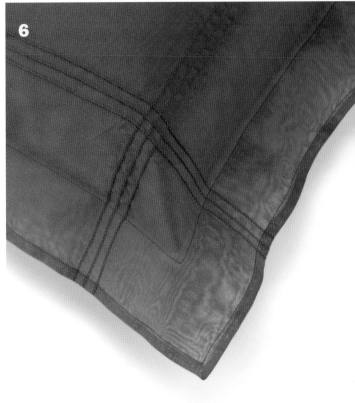

4 Pin the overlay front and back right sides together, and stitch ½" (1.3 cm) seam, including all four corners; leave a 14" (35.5 cm) opening on one side for turning and inserting the pillow. Trim the corners diagonally, ⅛" (3 mm) from the stitching. Trim the seams to ¼" (6 mm).

5 Turn the overlay right side out and press. Press under the seam allowances in the opening. Mark a line 2" (5 cm) from the outer edge. Topstitch on the marked line on the three sides that do not have the opening.

6 Insert the knife-edge pillow. Finish the topstitching, using a zipper foot to get close to the pillow. Slipstitch the outer opening closed. Topstitch ⅜" (1 cm) from the outer edge, encasing the raw edges.

Three on Three

This striking contemporary pillow features a trio of boldly colored silks accented with three knotted triplets of satin rattail cord. Because the side panels roll over the pillow's edges, to make the color blocks appear equally wide, the side rectangles are cut wider than the center one. The pillow back is prepared the same as the front but without the cord accents and with colors in the reverse order so they match across the outer seams. One of the back seams offers a convenient and inconspicuous place for a zipper closure.

1 Cut two 5¼" × 17" (13.2 × 43 cm) rectangles of each of two fabrics for the front and back side panels. Cut two 4½" × 17" (11.5 × 43 cm) panels of the third fabric for the front and back center panels.

2 Cut each cord into three 8" (20.5 cm) pieces. Tie three different cords together with a simple overhand knot. Center the knot across the middle of the center front panel; separate the cords and pin to the fabric edges. Take care not to draw in the sides of the panel. Repeat with two more cord sets, spacing the knots about 3½" (9 cm) apart.

3 Join the side panels to the center panel with ½" (1.3 cm) seams. Press the seam allowances open. Repeat for the back, inserting a zipper in one seam (page 23), if desired.

4 Finish the pillow following the directions for a knife-edge pillow (page 10). Take care to match up the seams between the front and back.

MATERIALS

¼ yd. (0.25 m) each of three bold-colored silks

⅔ yd. (0.63 m) each of three rattail cords to match silk colors

Thread to match fabrics

12" (30.5 cm) conventional zipper

12" × 16" (30.5 × 40.5 cm) pillow form

CLOSURE SUGGESTIONS

Invisible zipper in a back seam

Conventional zipper in a back seam

Invisible zipper in side seam

Around in Circles

This is not your grandmother's felt appliqué pillow. Basic embroidery stitches take on a new vibrancy in this happy explosion of color. The circles on this raw-edge flange pillow are hand-sewn using a method known as reverse appliqué, in which the holes are cut in the pillow front and the appliqués are placed underneath. All the fabrics are wool felts, which feel softer and have a richer appearance than ordinary craft felt. Matching pearl cotton yarns are used for the basic embroidery stitches that emphasize each circle. Have fun going around in circles!

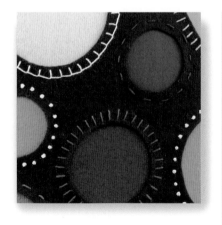

MATERIALS

Basic sewing supplies

⅝ yd. (0.6 m) dark wool felt for pillow front and back

¼ yd. (0.25 m) wool felt in each of five or six different bright colors

Marking chalk

Paper for making patterns

Compass for drawing circles

Thread and hand needle

#5 pearl cotton yarns to match felt circle colors

Crewel or chenille needle

16" (40.5 cm) square pillow form

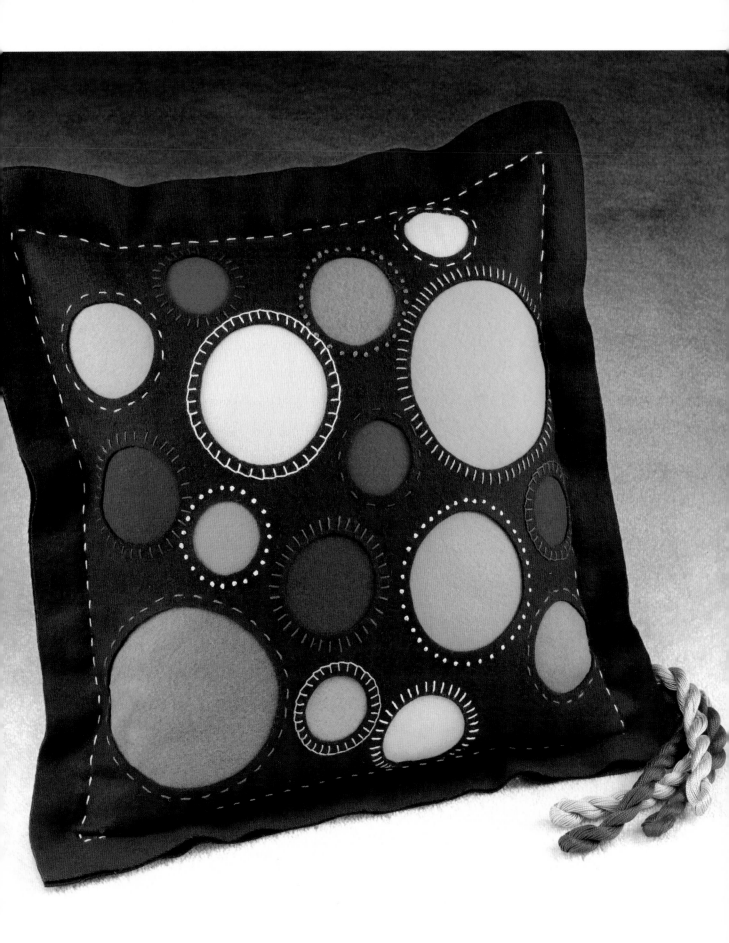

round in Circles

1 Cut two 19" (48.5 cm) squares for the pillow front and back. Set the back aside. Mark a square 1½" (3.8 cm) from the outer edge of the pillow front, using marking chalk.

2 Draw and cut out two paper circles each with 4½" and 3¼" (11.5 and 8.2 cm) diameters. Draw and cut out six circles each with 2½" and 1¾" (6.5 and 4.5 cm) diameters. Arrange the circles within the marked square, leaving at least a 1" (2.5 cm) margin around each circle. When you are pleased with your arrangement, mark the circles on the felt using chalk. Draw a simple diagram on paper, labeling each circle with the desired color.

4

Blanket stitch

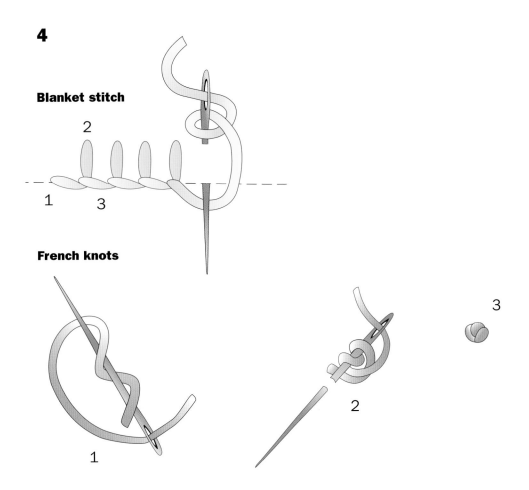

French knots

3 Pin the paper circles onto the desired colors of felt. Draw a 1/2" (1.3 cm) margin around each circle with chalk, and cut them out. Cut out the marked holes on the pillow front. Referring to your diagram, center each circle under the corresponding hole and hand-baste in place.

4 Work embroidery stitches around the edge of each circle, using a crewel needle and a single strand of pearl cotton, and securing the appliqués beneath the pillow front. We used a running stitch, blanket stitch, French knots, blanket stitch, and simple straight stitches set perpendicular to the circle edges. Remove the basting stitches.

5 Pin the pillow front and back wrong sides together. Remark the square with chalk, if necessary. Using a single strand of pearl cotton, stitch the layers together on the marked line with a running stitch. Leave one side open, but do not cut the pearl cotton.

6 Insert the pillow form. Finish stitching the last side.

Sashiko on Silk

Simple, yet beautiful, sashiko embroidery is a traditional Japanese needle art. An ancient technique for mending and reinforcing clothing, sashiko has become a modern fabric art for embellishing home décor items and exquisite garments. The stitch is quite humble—a simple running stitch—and easy enough for anyone to master. Because the technique is worked from the wrong side, it is a good idea to practice it before embroidering a pillow. Original sashiko was worked with white cotton thread on indigo-dyed cotton fabric. Today, the embroidery looks very sophisticated when stitched with silk floss on silk fabric. Typical sashiko designs are repetitive, interlocking patterns, often sold as quilting stencils. Sometimes the designs represent elements of nature or spiritualism. Nancy Shriber, a nationally recognized fiber artist, teacher, lecturer, and writer, designed and embroidered this silk sashiko pillow.

MATERIALS

Basic sewing supplies

1/2 yd. (0.5 m) indigo Thai silk for pillow

1/2 yd. (0.5 m) 100% cotton flannel

Quilting stencil in sashiko stitch grid

Pencil

Temporary fabric adhesive spray

Wooden embroidery hoop, 8" to 10" (20.5 to 25.5 cm) diameter

Twill tape or seam tape for wrapping hoop

Silk variegated embroidery floss

Thread conditioner such as Thread Heaven®

Hand embroidery needle, size 7 to 10

Padded pressing surface

1/2 yd. (0.5 m) lime green Thai silk for cording

1 yd. (0.92 m) cording

Thread to match fabric

Zipper or fasteners for closure as desired

3 yd. (2.75 m) ribbon yarn for tassel

Bead or charm

12" × 16" (30.5 × 40.5 cm) pillow form

CLOSURE SUGGESTIONS

Lapped back closure (plain or with fasteners)

Conventional zipper in pillow back

Sashiko on Silk

1 Cut 11" × 14" (28 × 35.5 cm) rectangles of indigo silk and flannel for the center panel of the pillow, running the slubs of the silk in the narrower direction. Mark a 9½" × 12" (24.3 × 30.5 cm) rectangle on the flannel, using a pencil. Transfer the sashiko design from the stencil onto the flannel.

2 Lightly spray the unmarked side of the flannel with temporary fabric adhesive. Layer the flannel, marked side up, over the wrong side of the silk.

3 Wrap the inner ring of the embroidery hoop with twill tape or seam tape to protect the fabric. Center the layered fabrics in the embroidery hoop; the fabrics should be taut but not stretched.

4 Separate out three strands of silk embroidery floss, about 18" (46 cm) long. Run the strands through thread conditioner, if desired. Thread the floss onto an embroidery needle and knot the end.

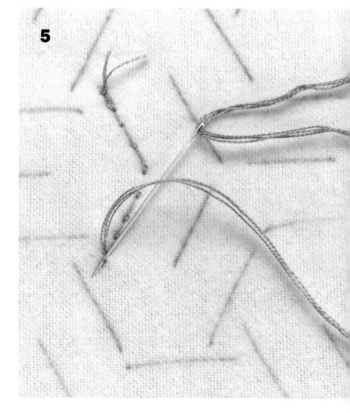

5 Take a small stitch at the beginning of a line near the center of the marked design. Take a small backstitch to lock the stitches. Then continue taking small running stitches along the marked design lines. Check the stitches on the right side of the silk; strive for consistent stitch length, about 1/8" (3 mm) long with consistent spacing between stitches. Backstitch in the flannel at the beginning and end of every design line to lock the stitches. Knot the floss in the flannel when it becomes too short, and begin again as in step 4.

6 Stitch all the design lines, working from the center outward to the marked rectangle. Move the embroidery hoop as necessary for stitching the outer areas. Remove the embroidered fabric from the hoop. Press lightly, facedown, on a padded pressing surface.

7 Cut the embroidered fabric 1/2" (1.3 cm) beyond the marked line. Cut two silk rectangles 41/4" × 13" (11.5 × 33 cm) with the slub of the silk running in the narrower direction.

8 Cut bias strips of the green silk, and prepare welting (page 30). You will need about 21/2 yd. (2.3 m) of welting. Stitch welting to the long sides of the sashiko panel, and then join a small silk rectangle to each of these sides.

9 Prepare the pillow back. Round the pillow front and back corners. Attach welting to the outer edge of the pillow front, and finish sewing the pillow together following the directions for a knife-edge pillow (page 10).

10 Make a 4" (10 cm) tassel, using ribbon yarn. Stitch a charm or bead to the tassel. Secure the tassel to the pillow top, just behind the welting, so it will dangle over the pillow front. Insert the pillow form.

Sun Prints

Harness the power of the sun to make bright, colorful pillows. Special sunlight-reactive Setacolor transparent paints by Pebeo are easy to use and create intriguing shadow images on fabric. If you just can't wait for a sunny day to print your fabric, you can use a halogen lamp or a sunlamp that emits ultraviolet light.

Fabric artist Diane Bartels designed this pillow using two fat quarters of commercially "hand-dyed" cotton quilt fabric, one for the sun print and one for the pillow back. Sun printing over hand-dyed or hand-painted fabric creates a design with lots of visual texture and color variation. Diane used a branch of sumac leaves from her backyard for her sun print. You can use any leaves or other opaque objects that lay fairly flat, such as twigs, feathers, coiled rope, or lace.

MATERIALS

Basic sewing supplies

Two fat quarters (18" × 22") commercially hand-dyed or hand-painted fabric for sun print, or 1/2 yd. (0.5 m) fabric, 45" (115 cm) wide

Hard, flat, portable surface, such as plywood, foam core, or heavy cardboard

Setacolor transparent paint in desired color; water

Container for mixing paint

Foam applicator

Opaque objects with interesting shapes for blocking the sun

Sunlight or other suitable light source

Washing machine and dryer

Oven and aluminum foil, optional

Iron

1/2 yd. (0.5 m) lining fabric

1/2 yd. (0.5 m) low-loft batting or flannel

Variegated thread for machine quilting

Zipper or fasteners for closure as desired

18" (46 cm) square pillow form

Thread to match fabric

CLOSURE SUGGESTIONS

Lapped back closure (plain or with fasteners)

Invisible zipper in outer seam

Sun Prints

1 Wet one fat quarter of fabric; wring out the excess water. Smooth out the fabric on the portable surface; secure the outer edges with pins or tape.

Tip: *The fabric doesn't have to be stretched taut. In fact, small wrinkles here and there will cause the paint to migrate and leave interesting color variations.*

2 Dilute the Setacolor transparent paint: two parts water to one part paint. Apply the paint to the fabric, using a foam applicator, covering the fabric completely.

3 Place opaque objects, such as pressed leaves, on the wet fabric. For best results, objects should lay flat on the fabric. Move the fabric to a sunny, still spot, where the objects will not be disturbed. Allow the fabric to dry completely.

4 Remove the objects. Heat-set the fabric by pressing from the wrong side at a temperature appropriate for the fabric. Or preheat the oven to 210° F (99° C), then turn off the oven, and place the fabric on aluminum foil in the oven for 10 minutes. Wash, dry, and press the fabric.

5 Square up the sun print to 18" × 18" (46 × 46 cm). Cut squares of batting or flannel and lining to the same size. Place the lining facedown. Smooth the batting or flannel over the lining; smooth the sun print, faceup, on top. Pin-baste the layers together.

6 Channel quilt the layers together, using variegated thread and stitching casual horizontal lines about 1" (2.5 cm) apart.

7 Cut, layer, and quilt the pillow back, if desired. Finish sewing the pillow together and insert the pillow form.

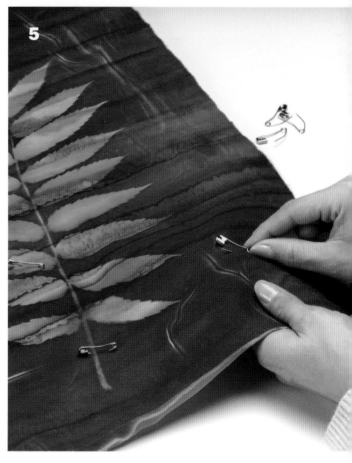

Foiled Design

A glistening foiled design adds an Asian element to this sophisticated, asymmetrical pillow. The character shown here means "happy." Three handcrafted buttons on a dark background panel are offset by a strip of beaded ball trim on the opposite side.

Any fabric can be foiled, though smoother surfaces yield clearer images. Products for foiling fabric (different from those used for foiling craft materials) are available at quilt shops, stores that specialize in textile arts, and Internet resources (page 158). A foiled pillow cover can be laundered but not dry cleaned.

MATERIALS

Basic sewing supplies

1/2 yd. (0.5 m) main fabric

1/4 yd. (0.25 m) contrasting fabric

Thread to match or blend with fabrics

Repositionable spray adhesive

Stencil

Foil transfer adhesive

Small foam applicator

Foil intended for use on fabric

Press cloth

1/2 yd. (0.5 m) beaded ball trim

Three decorative buttons, 1" (2.5 cm) in diameter

Zipper or fasteners for closure, as desired

12" × 16" (30.5 × 40.5 cm) pillow form

CLOSURE SUGGESTION

Invisible zipper in one end or bottom seam

$\mathcal{F}$oiled $\mathcal{D}$esign

1 Cut a 12" × 13" (30.5 × 33 cm) rectangle of the main fabric for the pillow front. Cut a 6" × 13" (15 × 33 cm) rectangle of the contrasting fabric. Stitch the pieces right sides together in a $1/2$" (1.3 cm) seam; press the seam allowances open. Mark a placement line for the beaded trim $41/2$" (11.5 cm) from the right edge of the pillow front.

2 Apply repositionable spray adhesive to the wrong side of the stencil. Allow to dry the length of time recommended by the manufacturer. Position the stencil on the pillow front, centered between the seam and the marked line.

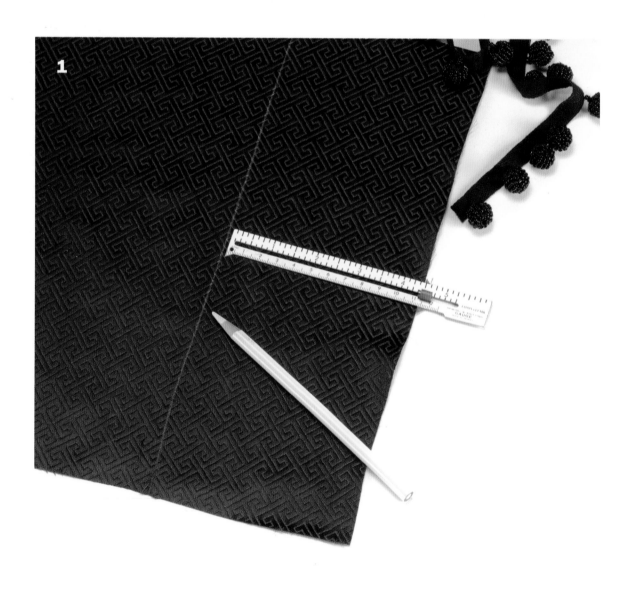

3

4

3 Apply foiling transfer adhesive to the fabric through the stencil, using a foam applicator in a dabbing or pouncing motion. Lift the stencil off the fabric, and wash the stencil immediately. Allow the adhesive to dry on the fabric following the manufacturer's instructions.

4 Place the foil, colored side up, over the fabric, and cover with a press cloth. Press with an iron set at high for ten seconds. Lift and reposition the iron as needed to cover the entire design. Allow to cool. Peel the cellophane backing away from the design.

5 Stitch the trim tape to the pillow front over the marked line, stitching down both sides. Use a zipper foot, if necessary, along the beaded side. Stitch the three buttons onto the contrasting section.

6 Prepare the pillow back. Finish the pillow following the directions for a knife-edge pillow (page 10). Insert the pillow form.

Hand-painted and Embossed

This exotic pillow was designed by Elaine Jackson, who also designs rubber stamps and needlework patterns. The pillow is an eclectic mix of embossed velvet and painted fabric accented with decorator trim. Shrink-plastic leaves dangle from velvet prairie points. You can copy her pillow to the last detail or substitute your own painted design and add different beads and charms.

Elaine's paint-pattern and three-step painting technique are easy, even for beginners. Painting on fabric is similar to painting on other surfaces, except the paint may absorb into the fabric more quickly. It is a good idea to practice on some fabric scraps, so you will know how wet to get the paint, how much paint to load on the brush, what kind of strokes work best, and how quickly the paint dries. When mixing colors for the skin and hair, mix enough paint to complete the entire area and reserve a little for mixing highlights.

MATERIALS

Basic sewing supplies

Copy machine

Light box or other glass surface with light coming through

1 yd. (0.92 m) white cotton muslin or broadcloth for painted panel and pillow form

Masking tape

Brushable matte fabric paint in colors: chocolate, ebony, golden tan, peach, glacier white, cool blue, berry red, olive, turquoise, and lime

Black permanent marker

Paintbrushes (medium round and small round)

Water

Paper plate or plastic palette

1 yd. (0.92 m) cognac-colored acetate/rayon velvet

Rubber stamp

Iron and firm ironing surface

Spray bottle with water

3/4 yd. (0.7 m) decorative fringe

Paper-backed two-sided clear adhesive

Invisible zipper, optional

Polyester fiberfill

Shrink plastic

Colored pencils

Eight wooden beads

Hole punch

Oven

CLOSURE SUGGESTION

Invisible zipper in bottom seam

Hand-painted and Embossed

1 Enlarge the painting pattern on page 71. Tape it to a light box or other glass surface with light coming through. Cut or tear two 12" × 18" (30.5 × 46 cm) rectangles of muslin. Layer them together over the pattern, and tape in place. Trace the pattern onto the fabric, using a black permanent marker.

2 Tape the layered fabric to a washable painting surface. Mix paint for the skin color, using chocolate, golden tan, peach, and white until the desired color is achieved. Water down slightly by dipping the paintbrush in water. Load the medium round brush and touch the paint to the center of the skin area. Fill in the large area quickly; use the smaller brush to fill in near the lines.

3 Paint the other areas in colors as shown. For the hair, mix chocolate with a tiny amount of ebony until the desired color is achieved. Paint the inner halves of the flower petals with berry red and the outer halves with peach, blending the two colors together where they meet. Allow the paint to dry.

4 For shading, water down the hair color until it is semitransparent. Using the smaller brush, shade the areas of the face that touch the flowers and the edge of the shirt. Shade the creases of the eyelid and left sides of the lines in the hair. Shade the outer edge of the sky area with watered-down turquoise.

5 Highlight the tops and centers of the leaves with lime green paint. Highlight the right side of the design lines in the hair and face and the outer lines of each flower petal, using their original colors mixed with glacier white.

6 Go over all the design lines again with the black marker. Add detail lines in the flowers, leaves, face, and eye. Allow to dry. Cut out the painted design, leaving 1/2" (1.3 cm) seam allowance all around.

7 Tear velvet into the following pieces: two 7¹/₂" × 13" (19.3 cm × 33 cm), one 13" × 23" (33 × 58.5 cm), and eight 4" (10 cm) squares.

8 Place a rubber stamp faceup on a firm ironing surface. Place a piece of velvet, facedown, over the stamp. Lightly mist the area of the velvet to be embossed.

9 Apply steady, even pressure with a hot, dry iron, pressing only in the area of the stamp. Reposition iron as necessary to cover the entire stamp and avoid leaving steam-hole impressions. Lift the iron straight up from the surface without disturbing the position of the velvet; hold for ten second in each area. Lift embossed velvet from the stamp.

15

10 Repeat steps 8 and 9 as many times as desired for each of the velvet pieces, changing the direction of the embossed images and running some of them off the edges.

11 Stitch the 7½" × 13" (19.3 cm × 33 cm) rectangles to the sides of the painted panel using ½" (1.3 cm) seam allowances. Press the seam allowances open. Secure the decorative trim over the seam, using paper-backed two-sided adhesive.

12 Fold each of the eight velvet squares in half diagonally and in half diagonally again, forming prairie points. Pin four prairie points to each narrow end of the pillow front, aligning the raw edges and overlapping as necessary. Baste within the ½" (1.3 cm) seam allowance.

13 Install an invisible zipper between the lower edges of the front and back, if desired. Place the pillow front and back, right sides together. Stitch ½" (1.3 cm) seam. Leave an opening for turning if you have not installed a zipper.

14 Make a 12" × 22" (30.5 × 56 cm) knife-edge pillow form (page 10) from muslin or broadcloth. Insert the form through the opening. Zip or slipstitch the pillow closed.

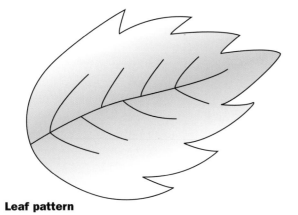

16

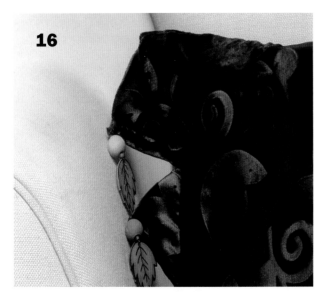

Leaf pattern

15 Trace the leaf pattern eight times onto shrink plastic using a black marker. Color the leaves on both sides, using colored pencils. Cut out the leaves and punch a ¼" (6 mm) hole near the base of each leaf. Shrink them in the oven, following the manufacturer's directions.

16 Stitch the leaf charms and wooden beads to the prairie points.

Painting pattern shown at 50%

No-sew Stamped Leather

You don't have to sew to make an awesome pillow. This unique leather pillow is made without a single stitch. The angled fringe encloses the pillow form with an ingenious system of slots and tabs. All you have to do is mark, cut, and insert. The falling leaves are stamped onto the leather using large foam stamps and metallic fabric paints. It is a good idea to test the stamping technique on a piece of cardboard or paper before applying it to the leather. Irregularities in the stamped images and variations in their color intensities only add to the character of the leaves.

MATERIALS

Two pieces of leather with 20" (51 cm) square usable area

Pencil

Ruler

Scissors

Masking tape

Craft knife and cutting surface

Metallic fabric paints in two different colors

Two different foam rubber leaf stamps

Two small foam applicators

16" (40.5 cm) pillow form

No-sew Stamped Leather

1 Mark a 20" (51 cm) square on the wrong side of each piece of leather, using a pencil. Cut out the squares. Mark off a 16" (40.5 cm) square in the center of each piece, using masking tape.

2 Use the template to mark the angled fringe sections on each side of the front and back, following the diagram. Mark the placement of each slit. Check for accuracy before cutting.

3 Cut the fringe using a scissors. Cut each slit, using a craft knife.

4 Apply fabric paint to one of the foam rubber stamps, using a foam applicator. Stamp the leather. Lift the stamp and repeat the process. Stamp a drift of leaves falling diagonally from one upper corner, alternating stamps and paint colors. Allow the paint to dry thoroughly.

5 Place the pillow front over the pillow back, wrong sides together. Insert the tabs from the front through the corresponding slits on the back; insert the tabs from the back through the corresponding slits on the front. Pull the tabs through as far as possible. Leave one side open.

6 Insert the pillow form. Insert tabs through slits to close the open side.

Template shown at 100%

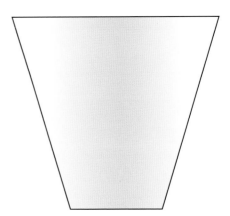

Front Diagram

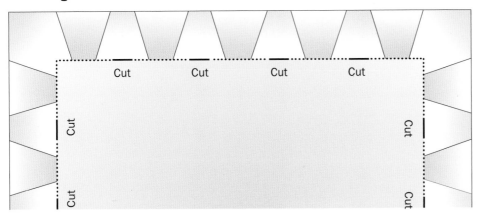

Back Diagram

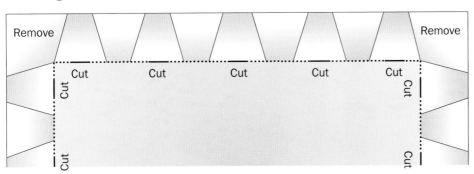

CHARMING & ROMANTIC

Here are some pillows to snuggle up to, caress, and daydream on. Some have nostalgic touches, like silk ribbon embroidery. Others, like the faux chenille and bubbled velvet pillows, are irresistibly soft and have calming colors. Satisfy your sentimental side with a few of these charming and romantic pillows.

Faux Chenille

The soft, watercolor look and inviting texture of this pillow are created by a technique known as faux chenille. Several layers of fabric are stitched together in channels running on the true bias of the fabric. The upper layers are slashed between the channels and then machine washed to fluff the fibers. The resulting fabric imitates a vintage, ribbed chenille bedspread. We used a cotton decorator print as the top fabric. Various solid color tones of the background color were selected for the underlayers. If you have fabric leftover from bedroom curtains or a duvet cover, you can turn it into a coordinating accent pillow for the bed.

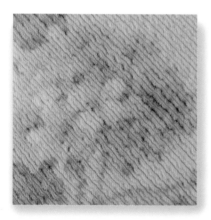

MATERIALS

Basic sewing supplies

⅝ yd. (0.6 m) cotton print decorator fabric for the pillow front top layer and the pillow back

⅝ yd. (0.6 m) each of three different cotton fabrics in values and tones of the decorator fabric background color for the underlayers

Pencil or removable fabric marker

Quilter's safety pins

Walking foot, optional

Quilting guide, optional

Thread to match fabric

Rotary slash cutter or small, sharp scissors

Zipper or fasteners for closure, as desired

Several bath towels of similar color to the fabrics

Washing machine and dryer

18" (46 cm) square pillow form

CLOSURE SUGGESTIONS

Lapped, centered back closure (plain or with fasteners)

Conventional zipper near one side in pillow back

Faux Chenille

1 Cut a 20" (51 cm) square of the decorator fabric for the pillow front, centering a large design motif and aligning the edges to the fabric grainlines. Cut 20" (51 cm) on-grain squares of the three underlayer fabrics.

2 Mark a line diagonally across the decorator fabric square. Stack the four fabrics, right sides up, and pin them together in several places, using quilter's safety pins.

3 Attach a walking foot, if you have one. Using a 2 mm straight stitch, stitch the fabrics together on the diagonal line. Use a quilting guide or gauge the space by watching the edge of the presser foot to stitch another line ⅜" (1 cm) from the first. Continue stitching diagonal lines ⅜" (1 cm) apart until the entire square is covered. Remove pins as you come to them.

4 Insert the slash cutter or scissors tips under the top three layers of fabric in the channel between two stitching lines. Slash the layers down the center of the channel. Continue, until all the channels have been slashed. Take care that you do not cut the bottom layer.

5 Recut the stitched layers to a 19" (48.5 cm) square. Prepare a 19" (48.5 cm) pillow back, and stitch it to the front, right sides together, following the directions for a knife-edge pillow (page 10). Turn it right side out.

6 Place the pillow cover, along with some towels of similar color, into the washing machine and wash in cool water with average agitation for ten minutes. Tumble dry. If the fibers are not sufficiently fluffed, repeat. Insert the pillow form.

3

4

Bonbons

Don't the balls on cotton ball fringe look like bonbons covered in powdered sugar? This simple knife-edge pillow of dotted satin is embellished with rows of fluffy ball fringe. You can design your pillow with one or more clusters of fringe rows like this one, or cover the entire pillow front with cotton balls. Either way, you will create a visual and tactile delight.

1 Cut two 13" × 17" (33 × 43 cm) rectangles for the pillow front and back. Cut a 13" (33 cm) strip of ball fringe, and pin it across the center of the pillow front. Stitch down both sides of the heading.

2 Cut two more strips of ball fringe to place on either side of the first strip, so that the balls will be even with the empty spaces of the first strip. Pin them in place, with the headings close together and fringe facing outward. Stitch down both sides of the headings.

3 Add two more strips on each side, staggering the balls to fill the empty spaces.

4 Prepare the pillow back with the desired closure (page 22). Sew the front to the back, following the directions for a knife-edge pillow (page 10). Insert the pillow form.

MATERIALS

1/2 yd. (0.5 m) dotted decorator satin

2 1/2 yd. (2.3 m) cotton ball fringe

Thread to match fabric

12" × 16" (30.5 × 40.5 cm) pillow form

Zipper or other fasteners, as desired

CLOSURE SUGGESTIONS

Lapped back closure with hook and loop tape or buttons

Conventional zipper in pillow back

Woven Ribbons and Tassels

Sheer and satin, sherbet-colored ribbons crisscross this fresh lemon-yellow pillow. The lavish ribbon and bead tassels at the corners look like they were found in an upscale design studio, but you can easily make them with common crafting materials. To help this knife-edge pillow support the weight of the tassels, shape the pillow corners, following steps 2 to 4 on page 10.

MATERIALS

Basic sewing supplies

⁵/₈ yd. (0.6 m) yellow crepe fabric

18" or 1 yd. (46 cm or 0.92 m) each of six to ten ribbons in a range of styles, widths, and colors

Thread to blend with fabric and ribbons

Removable tape

Invisible zipper or buttons for closure, as desired

4 yd. (3.7 m) narrow decorative cording

Four 20 mm glass beads

Four wooden craft flower pots, ⁵/₈" (1.5 cm) tall and wide

Hot glue gun

Wire hanger or other bendable wire

2 yd. (1.85 m) each of five ribbons in a range of styles and colors, ¹/₄" (7 mm) wide or narrower, for tassels

Tapestry needle

18" (46 cm) square pillow form

CLOSURE SUGGESTIONS

Invisible zipper in bottom seam

Lapped back closure with clear colored buttons to match ribbons

Woven Ribbons and Tassels

1 Cut an 18" (46 cm) square for the pillow front. Shape the corners as in steps 2 to 4 on page 10. Fold the front in half and press; refold in the opposite direction and press, to mark the center.

2 Cut the ribbons into 18" (46 cm) lengths. Arrange several ribbons across the pillow center, spacing them as desired. Pin the ribbons to the pillow at the outer edges.

3 Arrange the remaining ribbons across the pillow center in the opposite direction; pin at one end. Weave each ribbon through the first set and pin the loose end in place. Alternate the weave pattern with each ribbon, forming a simple basket weave.

4 Measure for accuracy and adjust placement of any ribbons as necessary. Baste the ribbons to the pillow front within the 1/2" (1.3 cm) seam allowance.

5 Tape the ribbons in place where they begin to weave together, using removable tape. Stitch along the outer edge of the outer ribbons in the center woven area. Remove the tape.

6 Prepare the pillow back. Use the front as a pattern for shaping the corners. Stitch the front to the back, right sides together, following the directions for a knife-edge pillow (page 10). Turn the pillow cover right side out.

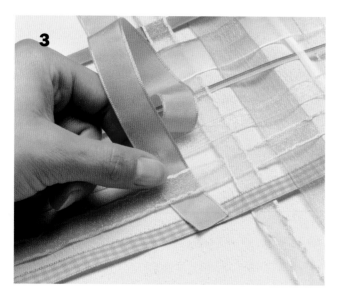

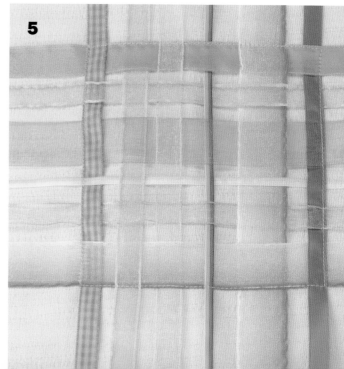

7 Cut a 10" (25.5 cm) piece of cording. Fold it in half and tie a knot halfway between the loop and the ends. String the cut ends through a bead and an inverted flower pot. Put a dot of hot glue between the bead and the flower pot; pull the cord ends so the knot is snug tight to the top of the bead and the bead adheres to the pot.

8 Hot-glue the cord ends to the outside of the flower pot.

9 Bend a wire hanger into a U shape with the sides about 5" (12.7 cm) apart. Wrap an 18" (46 cm) piece of narrow tassel ribbon around the wires, covering a space of about 2½" (6.5 cm). Tape the ends in place. Repeat with each of the remaining four tassel ribbons.

10 Stitch down the center of the wrapped ribbons. Remove the ribbon loops from the wires.

11 Fold the ribbon loops in half on the stitching line. Zigzag over the fold, forming a looped fringe.

12 Wrap the ribbon fringe around the flower pot; hot-glue in place. Wrap the upper edge of the fringe with decorative cording; secure with hot glue.

13 Repeat steps 7 to 12 three times to make four tassels. Thread the loop end of one tassel through a tapestry needle. Insert the needle between the stitches at one pillow corner and pull the tassel loop through to the inside of the pillow. Tie a large knot in the tassel loop tight against the corner stitches. Repeat at each remaining corner.

14 Insert the pillow form.

7

10

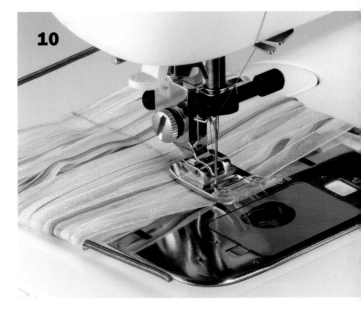

12

Ribbon Embroidery Sweetheart

This lovely heart-shaped box pillow is a perfect project to try the needle art of silk ribbon embroidery. Denise Giles, ribbon artist, designer, teacher, and demonstrator, designed the pillow using five basic ribbon embroidery stitches. Ribbon embroidery is very similar to embroidery with floss, and we'll tell you how to make the stitches. A key to successful ribbon embroidery is to let the ribbon float on the fabric surface rather than pulling it tight with each stitch.

MATERIALS

Basic sewing supplies

Tracing paper

Copy machine, optional

Masking tape

Light box

1/2 yd. (0.5 m) linen fabric

Disappearing fabric marker

Embroidery hoop

Medium beige-brown embroidery floss

Silk ribbons: two cards of 13-mm variegated pink, one card each of 13-mm variegated olive green, 4-mm light peach, 4-mm salmon, 4-mm pale grass green, and 4-mm medium green

Clear honey-colored seed beads

Embroidery needle

Beading needle

1 yd. (0.92 m) narrow twisted cord welting

Cording foot or zipper foot

Polyester fiberfill

$\mathcal{R}$ibbon $\mathcal{E}$mbroidery $\mathcal{S}$weetheart

1 Trace the embroidery pattern onto paper or copy it with a copy machine. Tape the pattern to a light box. Place a 15" (38 cm) square of linen, right side up, over the pattern. Trace the pattern onto the fabric, using a disappearing fabric marker.

2 Secure the fabric into an embroidery hoop. Stitch the design, following the stitch guide.

STITCH GUIDE

A. Stem Stitch using two strands of medium beige-brown embroidery floss.

B. Spider Web Rose using medium beige-brown embroidery floss and 13-mm variegated pink silk ribbon.

C. Lazy Daisy Stitch using 13-mm variegated pink silk ribbon.

D. French Knots using 4-mm salmon silk ribbon.

E. Lazy Daisy Stitch using 4-mm light peach silk ribbon.

F. Five Seed Beads in the center of each flower.

G. Japanese Ribbon Stitch using 13-mm variegated olive green silk ribbon.

H. Lazy Daisy Stitch using 4-mm pale grass green silk ribbon.

I. Japanese Ribbon Stitch using 4-mm medium green silk ribbon.

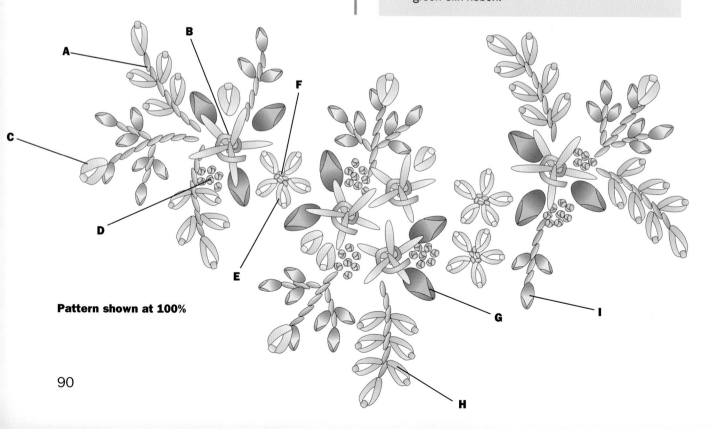

Pattern shown at 100%

3 Pin the pillow pattern over the embroidered square, centering the design. Cut out the pillow front; cut a matching pillow back. Attach narrow corded welting to the pillow front, using a cording foot or zipper foot and running the ends into the seam allowance at the top center of the heart. There is no need to retwist the ends together.

4 Cut a 32" × 3¼" (81.5 × 8.2 cm) boxing strip. Attach the boxing strip (page 18), following the instructions for a round pillow on the heart curves and for inside corners at the top center. Leave an opening on a straight back edge for stuffing.

5 Stuff the pillow with polyester fiberfill to the desired plumpness. Slipstitch the opening closed.

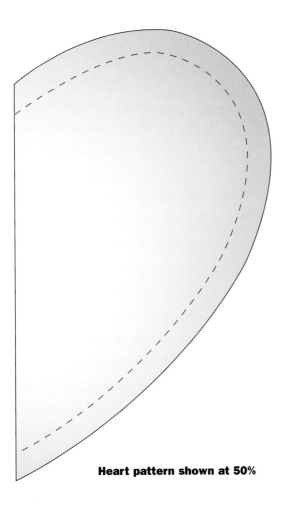

Heart pattern shown at 50%

RIBBON EMBROIDERY STITCHES

Spider Web Rose. Draw a circle with five evenly spaced spokes. Using embroidery floss, form a stitch along each of the spokes and tie off. Bring the ribbon up at the center of the web. Weave the ribbon over and under the spokes in an outward spiral until the spokes are covered and the rose is full. Keep the ribbon loose with occasional twists. Draw the ribbon through to the back and secure.

Lazy Daisy. Bring the needle up from the underside at the petal base; insert the needle right next to the exit point, and bring the needle back up at the petal tip. Pull the ribbon through the fabric, forming a small, smooth loop. Pass the ribbon over the loop; secure it with a small straight stitch at the petal tip.

Japanese Ribbon Stitch. Bring the needle and ribbon up from the underside. Smooth the ribbon flat in the direction of the stitch. Insert the needle at the end of the stitch, piercing the center of the ribbon. Pull the needle through to the underside until the ribbon curls inward at the tip. Take care not to pull the ribbon too tight.

French Knots. Bring the needle and ribbon up from the underside. Holding the needle parallel to the fabric near the exit point, wrap the ribbon once or twice around the needle; keep the ribbon smooth. Insert the needle very close to the exit point, holding the ribbon in place close to the wrapped needle. Hold the ribbon while pulling the needle through to the underside, releasing the ribbon as it disappears. The ribbon will form a soft knot.

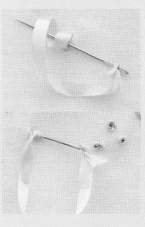

Satin Cloud

Fluffy clouds are for daydreaming, and so is this heavenly ruffled pillow. Its spiral of luxurious satin ruffles begs to be touched. This project is much easier than it looks because the ruffles are made of satin blanket binding, which comes with finished edges. Blanket binding is sold in a rainbow of colors, so you can make ruffled pillows in other colors, too.

MATERIALS

Basic sewing supplies

Paper for making the pattern

Compass or string, pushpin, ruler, and pencil

Black marker

1/2" yd. (0.5 m) firm satin

Zipper or fasteners for closure, as desired

Disappearing fabric marker

Three packages satin blanket binding, 4³/4 yd. (4.35 m) each

Thread to match fabric

14" (35.5 cm) round pillow form

CLOSURE SUGGESTIONS

Lapped, centered back closure (plain or with fasteners)

Conventional zipper centered in pillow back

$\mathcal{S}$atin $\mathcal{C}$loud

1 Draw a 15" (38 cm) circle on paper and cut it out. Fold the circle into fourths. Measuring from the center point, mark an arc every ¾" (2 cm) on one section; darken the lines with a black marker. Open out one fold, and use the darkened lines to trace arcs on the adjoining section. Repeat in the third section. In the fourth section, connect the inner arc to the second, the second to the third, etc., out to the last arc. Draw the last arc to trail off the edge. This will create a pattern with a continuous spiral.

2 Cut a 15" (38 cm) circle for the pillow front from the satin. Place the front, right side up, over the pattern. Trace the spiral onto the pillow front, using a disappearing fabric marker.

3 Join the three lengths of blanket binding using narrow French seams: stitch two ends wrong sides together with ⅛" (3 mm) seam; press to one side. Fold in the opposite direction with right sides together and the seam on the edge. Stitch again at slightly more than ⅛" (3 mm) depth, encasing the raw edges; press to one side.

1

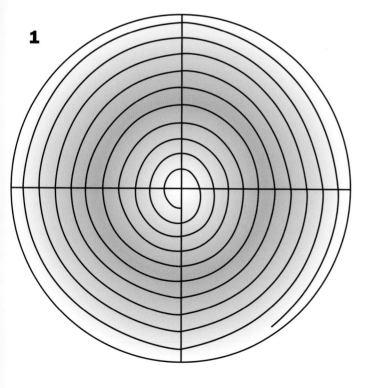

3

4 Finish one end with a narrow hem: fold under ¼" (6 mm), and edgestitch along the fold. Trim close to the stitches. Turn under the stitched edge, and edgestitch again, encasing the raw edge.

5 Unfold the blanket binding. Sew a basting stitch down the center fold for gathering. Working from the shiny side, secure the gathering thread at the hemmed end by winding it around a pin in a figure eight. Pull up the gathering thread 1 yd. (0.92 m) away, and gather the first section of blanket binding to 18" (46 cm); secure the thread. Repeat, gathering the entire length of binding to double fullness, one yard at a time.

6 Stitch the gathered binding to the marked spiral on the pillow front, beginning in the center. With the shiny side up, stitch down the center of the binding, over the gathering stitches. As you approach each pin, remove the pin and hold the loops of the gathering thread to the side until you have stitched beyond them and they have been caught under the new stitches. Wait to cut them until you are finished stitching. Continue to the end of the spiral, allowing the excess binding to trail off the edge. Cut the end 1" (2.5 cm) beyond the pillow edge.

7 Prepare the pillow back. If it will have a closure, follow the cutting directions for the closure style (page 22). Stitch the back to the front to complete the pillow, following the directions for a knife-edge pillow (page 10). Take care not to catch the outer row of ruffles in the seam. Insert the pillow form.

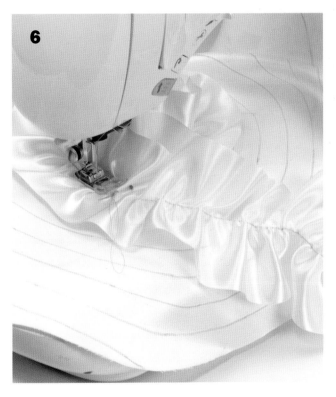

*B*ubbled *V*elvet

Washed velvet is luxuriously soft and has a vintage romantic look that makes it perfect for a boudoir. The fascinating bubbled texture of this bolster is created by poking the fabric through a raised metal grid, such as a kitchen cooling rack! For a 16" × 5" (40.5 × 12.7 cm) bolster, as seen here, you will need a 16" (40.5 cm) square of bubbled fabric. If your grid is smaller, bubble the fabric in sections.

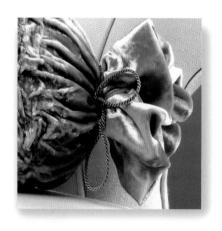

Materials

Basic sewing supplies

1 yd. (0.92 m) washed velvet

*Raised wire grid with 3/4" (2 cm) spaces,
such as a kitchen cooling rack*

Spray bottle and water

1/2 yd. (0.5 m) paper-backed fusible adhesive sheet

1/2 yd. cotton muslin

Thread to match fabric

2 yd. (1.85 m) narrow decorative cording

6" × 5" (15 × 12.7 cm) bolster pillow form

Bubbled Velvet

1 Place a full-width, 1-yd. (0.92 m) piece of washed velvet facedown over a slightly raised wire grid, with the lower cut edge extending 2" (5 cm) off the grid on the side closest to you. Spray the center area of the velvet (about 32" [81.5 cm] wide) with water, until it is damp.

2 Poke the fabric down into each hole of the first row of the grid, beginning at the center and working outward in both directions. Control the fabric with your fingers. The cut edge closest to you should extend evenly at least 1" (2.5 cm).

3 Poke the fabric into the holes of the next row, working from the center outward, without pulling the fabric from the first row. Fill each successive row, working through the entire grid. Fill all the holes equally, and keep the fabric on-grain. The center area of the fabric will shrink up to about half its size. Allow the fabric to dry in the grid.

4 Cut a 17" (43 cm) square of paper-backed fusible adhesive and an 18" (46 cm) square of muslin. Fuse the adhesive to the muslin. Trim the muslin even with the fusible adhesive.

5 Remove the paper backing, and place the muslin, fusible side down, over the velvet in the grid so the lower edge and one side of the muslin extend ½" (1.3 cm) beyond the lower edge and side of the grid. Fuse in place.

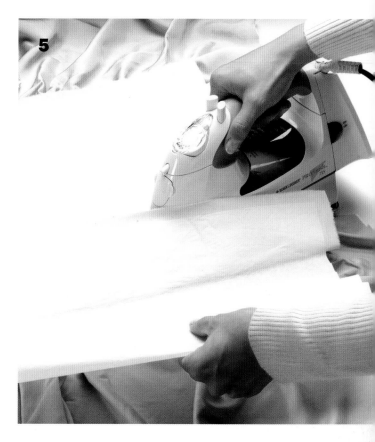

6 Gently remove the fused bubbled fabric from the grid. If the grid is not large enough to accommodate the 17" (43 cm) square, reposition it with the uppermost row of bubbles in the lower row of the grid. Dampen the unbubbled area and repeat steps 2 and 3 for the number of rows necessary. Then fuse the rest of the muslin in place.

7 Stitch around the outer edge of the bubbled square from the right side. You will be stitching ½" (1.3 cm) from the edge of the muslin.

8 Trim the velvet even with the muslin in the crosswise direction, cutting with scissors along the muslin and tearing the velvet from the corners of the muslin to the selvages. (The velvet will tear on grain.) Trim away the selvages of the velvet 9" (23 cm) from the muslin.

9 Complete the pillow following the directions for a candy wrapper bolster, steps 2 to 4 on page 20.

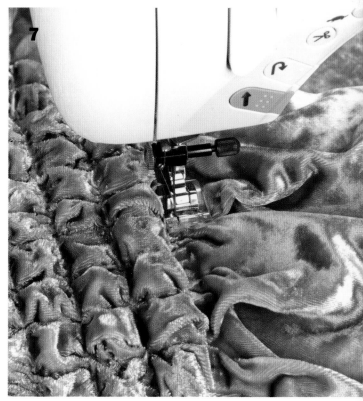

CLASSIC & NEW

The pillows in this section are updated interpretations of classic styles. Each features a fabric, trim, or technique that you can easily adapt for your own décor. Made with luxurious silks and wools, and extravagant fringes and beads, these pillows will give your home a touch of sophistication and elegance.

Timeless Toile

Classic toile fabrics make interesting pillows because of the stories they tell. Their intricate one-color designs, printed on white or cream backgrounds, depict historical events, country scenes, or exotic places. Typically, a toile fabric includes several different designs that are repeated across the fabric. You can create an interesting pillow assortment by centering a different design on the front of each pillow. On these knife-edge pillows, the toile is outlined with thin black welting and then framed with fabrics in black and white checks and nubby, textured stripes—all in silk. Narrow black box-pleated trim is sewn into the outer seams for a neat, tailored finish.

Two styles are shown. The directions on page 104 and 105 are for the pillow with the on-point motif, which, because of its bias seamlines, is a little trickier than the rectangular pillow. For the 14" × 18" (35.5 × 46 cm) rectangular pillow, make the center panel wide enough to accommodate the desired toile motif, and follow the general directions.

MATERIALS

For Square Pillow

Basic sewing supplies

Tissue paper for making the pattern

1/2 yd. (0.5 m) checked fabric

1/2 yd. (0.5 m) toile fabric (more may be needed to center the desired image)

2 yd. (1.85 m) narrow black piping

Thread to match fabric

Piping foot or zipper foot

2 1/8 yd. (1.95 m) narrow pleated trim

Liquid fray preventer

3/4 yd. (0.7 m) striped or checked fabric for pillow back

Zipper or fasteners for closure, as desired

18" (46 cm) square pillow form

For Rectangular Pillow

Tissue paper for making the pattern

1/2 yd. (0.5 m) toile fabric (more may be needed to center the desired image)

3/4 yd. (0.7 m) striped fabric for side panels and pillow back

1 yd. (0.95 m) narrow black piping

Piping foot or zipper foot

Zipper or fasteners for closure as desired

14" × 18" (35.5 × 46 cm) pillow form

CLOSURE SUGGESTIONS

Lapped back closure (plain or with fasteners)

Conventional zipper in pillow back

Invisible zipper in bottom seam of rectangular pillow

Timeless Toile

1 Draw a pattern with the finished measurements of the pillow front. Mark the centers of each side and connect the marks with straight lines. Cut the pattern apart on the lines. Use the pieces to draw new pattern pieces on tissue paper, adding ½" (1.3 cm) seam allowances around each piece.

2 Pin the triangle patterns to the checked fabric with the square corners of the triangles on the straight grain. Cut out the pillow corners. Center the square pattern, on point, over the right side of the toile design. Cut out the center.

3 Cut lengths of piping, using the pattern pieces as guides. Note that the edges to which the piping will be applied are on the bias. The piping pieces will act as a guide to ensure the fabric edges remain the correct length. Remove 1" (2.5 cm) of cording from the ends of each piping piece to reduce bulk where the seams will cross.

4 Pin the piping to the right side of the bias edge of one corner piece, aligning the piping seam to the ½" (1.3 cm) seamline. Stitch; using a piping foot or zipper foot.

5 Pin the corner piece to one edge of the center panel, right sides together. With the wrong side of the corner facing up, stitch the seam, stitching just inside the first stitches. Press the corner piece and seam allowances away from the center.

6 Repeat steps 4 and 5 at the opposite corner and then at the two remaining corners. Stitch the pleated trim to the outer edge. Apply liquid fray preventer to the cut ends, and overlap them slightly. Prepare the pillow back and finish sewing the pillow together, following the directions for a knife-edge pillow (page 10). Insert the pillow form.

*B*eaded *W*ave *P*leats

Waves of narrow pleats sewn down the pillow front play up the lustrous sheen of silk fabric. The pleats are stitched down in alternating directions and accented with coppery glass beads. Welted edges along the mini-plaid boxing strip are pinched together at the corners and held with strands of beads for high-style detailing.

MATERIALS

Basic sewing supplies

1 yd. (0.92 m) silk fabric for front, back, and welting

Chalk fabric marker

Thread to match fabrics

Zipper or fasteners for closure, as desired

4 yd. (3.7 m) cording for welting

1/2 yd (0.5 m) coordinating mini-plaid silk for boxing strip

120 copper-colored faceted glass beads, 4 mm in diameter

18" (46 cm) square pillow form

CLOSURE SUGGESTIONS

Conventional zipper centered in one side of boxing strip

Lapped, centered back closure (plain or with fasteners)

Beaded Wave Pleats

1 Cut the pillow front 17" × 23" (43 × 58.5 cm). Using a chalk fabric marker, mark a series of four lines, 1" (2.5 cm) apart, starting 4" (10 cm) from each of the short sides. Mark a third series of four lines in the center of the pillow front.

2 Fold the fabric at the first line, wrong sides together, and press a crease; unfold. Repeat for the remaining lines.

3 Refold the first crease. Stitch ¼" (6 mm) from the fold, forming a narrow pleat. Repeat for the remaining creases, forming three sets of narrow pleats.

4 Turn the outer pleats of each set outward and the inner pleats inward, along the raw edges. Baste the pleat ends in place within the ½" (1.3 cm) seam allowance.

5 Cut the pillow back 17" (43 cm) square. Or, if the back will have a closure, follow the cutting directions for the closure style (page 22). Prepare the pillow back. Prepare welting (page 30) and stitch it to the outer edges of the front and back. Cut the boxing strip (page 17) 3½" (9 cm) wide; attach it to the front and back.

6 Stitch a bead at the point where the folds of the two center pleats in each set meet near the outer edges. Hand-tack together the folds of the same two pleats at 4" (10 cm) intervals; stitch a bead at each point.

7 Hand-tack together the folds of the two outer pleats in each set, 2" (5 cm) from the ends; stitch a bead at each point. Hand-tack together the folds of the same two pleats at 4" (10 cm) intervals, and stitch beads at each point. Turn the outer pleats outward at points even with the beads of the inner pleats; hand-tack in place, and stitch beads at each point.

8 Insert the pillow form. Thread a needle with a double strand of thread, and knot the end. Tack an upper and lower corner of the welting together. String five or six beads onto the thread and stitch them over the corner; repeat twice. Repeat with three strands at each corner.

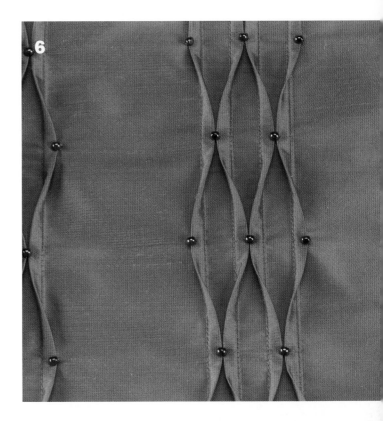

Framed Image

Handcrafting and computer technology can come together to create a one-of-a-kind pillow. The center panel is a photograph printed on special fabric. Fabric for the photo "frame" and pillow back is selected to echo a color in the photograph—in this pillow the warm chestnut brown of the horses. The long, black, shaggy fringe recalls the horses' manes. Choose any photograph and select complementary fabrics and trims.

Printable fabric sheets are available at computer supply stores and many quilt shops. The fabric is pretreated with an ink fixative and temporarily bonded to paper for smooth feeding through an ink-jet printer. The image is printed directly onto cotton fabric, which remains soft and pliable.

MATERIALS

Basic sewing supplies

Photograph

Computer, scanner, and ink-jet printer

Printable fabric sheets

1/8 yd. (0.15 m) black fabric for narrow trim around the photo

Thread to match fabric

1/2 yd. (0.5 m) faux suede fabric for the pillow back and front borders

1 1/2 yd. (1.4 m) fringe

Masking tape

Zipper or fasteners for closure as desired

12" × 16" (30.5 × 40.5 cm) pillow form

CLOSURE SUGGESTIONS

Invisible zipper in bottom seam

Conventional zipper centered or near one side in pillow back

Framed Image

1 Scan the photo at 300 DPI resolution or higher or use a digital image. Enlarge it to 8" × 10" (20.5 × 25.5 cm). Open the image within the software application of your choice; center it on the page. Adjust the colors, if necessary.

2 Under File, select Print. Click on the Properties button. Select Best for the Print Quality and Plain Paper for the Paper Type. Print a test of the photo on plain paper to check the image quality and placement. Make adjustments to the colors, if necessary, and try other print settings until you get the desired results.

3 Remove the plain paper from the tray and insert one sheet of the printable fabric. (For most front-loading printers, the fabric should face down.) Print the image.

5

4 Allow the ink to dry thoroughly. Remove the paper backing. Follow the manufacturer's instructions for rinsing the printed fabric, if necessary.

5 Cut two 8½" × 1¾" (21.8 × 4.5 cm) strips and two 11" × 1¾" (28 × 4.5 cm) strips of the black fabric. Fold them in half lengthwise; press. Align the raw edges of the short strips to the short edges of the printed fabric, right sides together. Baste within the ½" (1.3 cm) seam allowance. Repeat with the long strips on the long edges, forming a "matting" for the photo.

6 Cut two 4" × 8½" (10 × 21.8 cm) and two 3½" × 17" (9 × 43 cm) border pieces from the faux suede. Align the raw edges of the short borders to the short edges of the printed fabric, right sides together. Stitch ½" (1.3 cm) seams, encasing the matting between the frame and the photo. Lightly press the borders away from the photo and matting. Repeat with the longer border pieces.

7 Pin the fringe to the pillow front, with the upper edge of the fringe heading 1" (2.5 cm) from the outer edge of the pillow. Miter the fringe at the corners and overlap the ends. Stitch along the upper edge of the heading.

8 Weaken the adhesive side of masking tape by touching it to a fabric surface a few times. Turn the fringe back away from the outer edge of the pillow front, and tape in place with the weakened tape.

9 Prepare the pillow back, and stitch it to the front to complete the pillow, following the directions for a knife-edge pillow (page 10). Turn the pillow cover right side out and carefully remove the masking tape. Insert the pillow form.

7

8

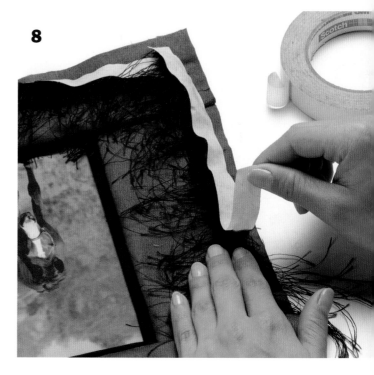

Elegant Foursome

Interior design studios carry lots of pieced pillows with a rich custom-designed look and price tags to match, but it doesn't take a degree in interior design or an unlimited budget to create one. Selecting the fabrics and trims is easy because manufacturers offer color-coordinated "families" of decorator fabrics in a variety of prints and textures. Start by choosing one fabric that has all the colors you want to work with, such as the striped fabric in this pillow. Then choose three more fabrics that repeat the colors in different textures, print types, and scales. To accent the seams, select a flat braid trim. Then find a plush multicolored fringe for the outer edges. As a finishing touch for our high-style pillow, we also added a chenille cord at the base of the fringe.

MATERIALS

Basic sewing supplies

Paper and tissue paper for making the pattern

1/4 yd. (0.25 m) fabric or remnants of three coordinating fabrics

1/2 yd. (0.5 m) fabric for the pillow back and one section of the front

Thread to match or blend with the fabrics

1 yd. (0.92 m) or more flat braid trim

2 yd. (1.85 m) fringe

Zipper or fasteners for closure, as desired

2 yd. (1.85 m) cording, optional

Liquid fray preventer and fabric glue for securing cording, optional

16" (40.5 cm) square pillow form

CLOSURE SUGGESTIONS

Lapped, centered back closure (plain or with fasteners)

Conventional zipper centered or near one side in pillow back

Elegant Foursome

1 Make a pattern by drawing a 16" (40.5 cm) square on a piece of paper. Draw seamlines dividing the square into four unequal rectangles. Plan which fabric will be used for each section; number the sections in the order they will be sewn. Draw match marks across the seamlines between adjoining sections. Cut out the square and cut it apart at the seamlines. Trace the rectangles onto tissue paper and add ½" (1.3 cm) seam allowances around each piece. Transfer the match marks.

2 Cut out the fabric sections, using the patterns as guides. Make shallow clips in the fabric edges at the match marks.

3 Pin sections 1 and 2, right sides together. Stitch ½" (1.3 cm) seam. Press the seam open. Center a strip of flat braid trim over the right side of the seam. Stitch down the center.

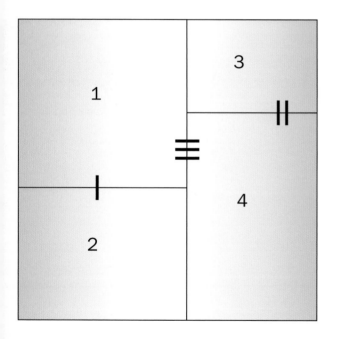

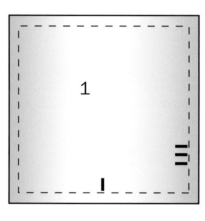

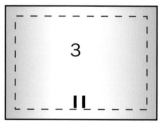

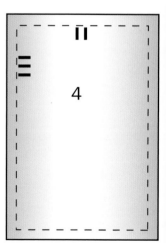

4 Repeat step 3 for the next set of adjoining rectangles. Continue until the pillow front is complete.

5 Attach fringe (page 34) to the outer edge of the front. If the back will have a closure, follow the cutting directions for the closure style (page 22). Prepare the pillow back, and stitch it to the front, following the directions for a knife-edge pillow (page 10).

6 To apply optional cording, separate the cording from the attached tape. Measure the length needed and mark the beginning and end with pins. Saturate the cording around the marks with liquid fray preventer; allow to dry. Cut the cording. Secure the cording to the pillow at the base of the fringe, using fabric glue and butting the ends together at an inconspicuous spot along the bottom.

7 Insert the pillow form.

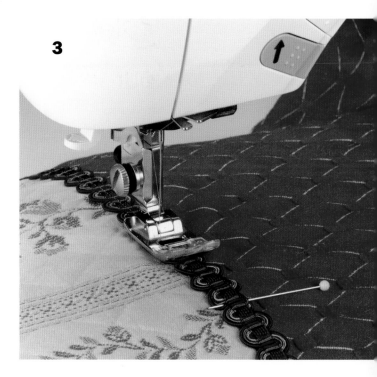

Fur Bolster with Ties

Many faux furs are so realistic, it's hard to tell them from real fur. The fibers are thick and long, often sculpted to look like rows of pelts sewn together. Faux fur has a nap, which means it brushes flat in one lengthwise direction, like a real animal coat. The "hairs" of the fur we chose were dyed dark at the "roots" and light at the ends, so the fabric has intriguing texture and depth as it curves around the bolster and ripples at the ends. The playful fur balls at the ends of the satin cords are made by covering Ping-Pong balls. Everyone who sees this pillow just has to pet it.

Faux furs are stable knit fabrics with a long, dense pile, so they have a bit of stretch in the crosswise direction and the cut edges won't ravel. Sewing faux fur is as easy as sewing any knit fabric. The only tricky part is dealing with the added bulk of the fur. The techniques used for sewing this pillow minimize the bulk at the seams and turned edges, and make seams as invisible as possible.

MATERIALS

Basic sewing supplies

Neckroll bolster pillow form

Faux fur, amount equal to the circumference of the pillow form

Chalk marking pencil

Appliqué scissors, optional

Thread to match fabric

Seam ripper or small crochet hook

Awl

Candle

Four Ping-Pong balls

2 yd. (1.85 m) satin rattail cord

Tape

Long upholstery needle

Bodkin

Fabric glue

Fur Bolster with Ties

1 Measure the circumference of the pillow form. Mark a rectangle on the wrong side of the faux fur with the circumference measurement running in the lengthwise direction of the fur. The width should be 1½" (3.8 cm) wider than the sum of the form length and the diameter of one end. Cut out the rectangle, cutting through only the base fabric with the tips of the shears. In this way, you avoid cutting the fur.

2 "Shave" off the fur from the base fabric ¾" (2 cm) from the lengthwise edges. One way to do this is to use an appliqué scissors, keeping the lower blade flat against the base fabric. It is easiest to work against the nap of the fur, a little at a time.

3 Turn under the shaved edges ¾" (2.5 cm) and stitch from the wrong side, ¼" (6 mm) from the cut edge, forming a casing at each side. From the right side, gently free any fur fibers that are caught under the stitches, using the tip of a seam ripper or a small crochet hook.

4 Shave off the fur from the base fabric ¼" (6 mm) from both crosswise edges. Pin the edges right sides together, pushing the fur away from the edges. Stitch ¼" (6 mm) seam, beginning and ending at the outer stitching lines, forming a tube.

5 Turn the tube right side out. Gently free any fur fibers that are caught under the stitches of the crosswise seam, and smooth it down. Slip the pillow form into the tube and center it.

6 Hold the tip of an awl in a candle flame to heat it. Melt two holes on opposite sides of each Ping-Pong ball.

7 Cut the rattail cord into two 1-yd. (0.92 m) lengths. Wrap the ends with tape to stiffen them, and cut them diagonally into points. Insert the tip of a long upholstery needle under the tape on one end and use it to guide the rattail into and through a Ping-Pong ball. Remove the needle and tie a knot in the cord end. Repeat for the second cord.

8 Thread the cords through the casings, using a bodkin.

9 Thread the free cord ends through the other Ping-Pong balls as in step 7, and knot the ends. Cut three tiny snips in the edges of the holes on the knot sides of the balls. Pull on the cords to pull the knots inside the balls.

10 Trace and cut out the ball-cover pattern. Place the pattern on the back of the fur, aligning the arrow to the lengthwise direction with the nap running toward the bottom. Trace the pattern with chalk and cut it out, cutting as in step 1. Repeat three times.

11 Apply fabric glue to the ball cover back. Adhere it to the Ping-Pong ball, wrapping it so the bottom points meet to cover the bottom hole and the top points snug up against the cord. Repeat for each ball.

12 Pull the cords tightly to close the bolster, and tie in a bow.

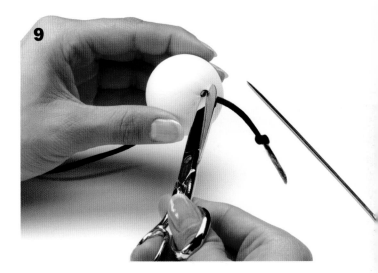

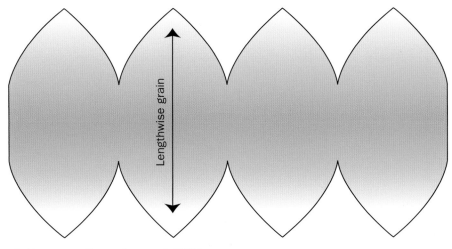

Lengthwise grain

Ball cover pattern shown at 100%

Rug Hook on Burlap

The primitive floral design on this pillow is created by looping thin strips of wool through a burlap background with a needle-art method known as rug hooking. Traditional rug-hooking designs cover the surface completely, but an outline design like this one takes much less time. The rustic, natural quality of the background fabric becomes part of the pillow styling. The narrow flange is wrapped with strands of yarn that echo the colors of the leaves and flowers.

This pillow was designed and hooked by Teresa Henn, an avid rug hooker and expert sewer who made many of the pillows in this book. Teresa's design of meandering vines and simple flowers resembles Jacobean embroidery.

MATERIALS

Basic sewing supplies

Copy machine

1/2 yd. (0.5 m) nylon netting for transferring design

Permanent marker

3/4 yd. (0.7 m) decorator burlap

Masking tape

Thread to match fabric

6" × 18" (15 × 46 cm) mediumweight, hand-dyed, 1005 wool in five colors

Rotary cutter, cutting mat, and heavy clear plastic ruler

Rug-hooking frame or wooden quilting hoop

Rug hook in primitive size

1/2 yd. (0.5 m) mediumweight wool for pillow back

Buttons for back closure, optional

Eight to ten lengths of wool tapestry yarn in each design color for the pillow border

No. 16 tapestry needle

16" (40.5 cm) square pillow form

CLOSURE SUGGESTION

Lapped, centered back closure (plain or with rustic buttons)

Rug Hook on Burlap

1 Enlarge the design. Trace the design, including grainlines, onto nylon netting, using a permanent marker.

2 Cut a 25" (63.5 cm) square of burlap, cutting the sides perfectly on grain. Fold masking tape around the raw edges to prevent raveling. Mark a 17½" (44.3 cm) square in the center of the burlap, following yarns in the weave. Zigzag around the marked square, stitching over two or three yarns.

3 Center the netting pattern over the burlap inside the square; pin. Trace the design onto the burlap by drawing through the netting, using the marker.

4 Cut ¼" (6 mm) lengthwise strips of the rug-hooking wool using a rotary cutter, heavy plastic ruler, and cutting mat.

5 Secure the burlap in a frame or hoop; it should be very taut.

6 Hold the rug hook in the palm of your hand above the design, with the hook turned up. Hold the wool strip between the thumb and forefinger of the opposite hand; this hand will be held beneath the frame and will guide the wool strip, making sure it does not twist.

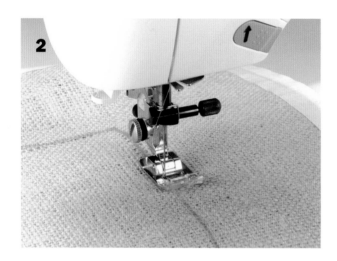

Pattern shown at 25%

7 Push the rug hook down through a hole in the burlap at the beginning of a design line, and catch the wool strip in the hook. Pull the end of the strip to the right side, to a height of about 1" (2.5 cm).

8 Continue hooking the wool strip, skipping a hole in the burlap between each insertion of the rug hook. Pull the wool loops to a height of about ¼" (6 mm). Space the loops evenly, with no gaps between them and avoid twisting the wool strip.

9 End each strip by pulling it through to the front. Insert the rug hook into the same opening to begin another strip. Clip ends of strips even with the loops when each design area is completed, taking care not to clip the loops.

3

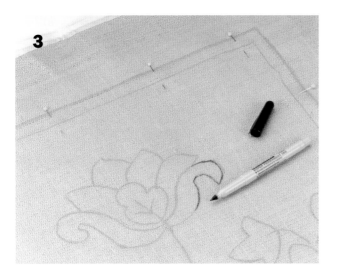

8

10 Cut the pillow front just beyond the zigzag stitches. Prepare the pillow back with a centered, lapped closure (page 26); make it the same size as the front. Stitch the front to the back, right sides together, 1/4" (6 mm) from the edges. Trim the corners diagonally; turn right sides out and press the outer edges.

11 Separate the tapestry yarns into three strands each. Thread one strand of each color together through a tapestry needle. Take a small stitch in the outer margin near the hooked edge. Insert the needle near the hooked edge on the front, pull the needle out the back, and wrap the yarn over the edge. Repeat, working in the direction of the yarn tails and covering them with the stitches.

12 Continue whipstitching in this manner around the entire pillow. Keep the yarns perpendicular to the edge and space the stitches close enough to hide the fabric. When you run out of yarn, take a small stitch in the burlap and hide the tails under the whipstitches. Begin again by hiding the tails of the new strands under the stitches. Miter the stitches at the corners, as shown.

13 Insert the pillow form.

11

12

Woven Wool Collage

Make a dramatic accent for your living room with a woven wool collage pillow. The large and small multicolored squares are created with a technique called random-cut fabric weaving, in which several fabrics are cut into wavy strips, interwoven, and stitched together. The pillow front is constructed much like Elegant Foursome on page 114, using the woven piece as the focus fabric. If you enjoy free-motion quilting, show off some of your skills on the solid wool rectangles; otherwise they can be left plain.

MATERIALS

Basic sewing supplies

Fusible knit interfacing for foundation, 20" × 24" (51 × 61 cm)

Padded pinning board or foam-core board

Four or more wool fabrics, about 1/2 yd. (0.5 m) each

Rotary cutter and cutting mat

Press cloth

Thread to coordinate with the fabrics

Muslin backing and batting for quilting solid blocks, if desired

1/2 yd (0.5 m) each of two flat decorator trims

1/2 yd. (0.5 m) velvet ribbon, 7/8" (23 mm) wide

Invisible zipper, optional

Four tassels

20" (51 cm) square pillow form

CLOSURE SUGGESTION

Invisible zipper in bottom seam

Woven Wool Collage

1 Smooth the interfacing, fusible side up, onto the pinning board. Secure with pins around the outer edges, keeping the interfacing taut but not stretched.

2 Using a rotary cutter, cut a wool strip of the desired width with irregular wavy edges to fit the foundation diagonally near the center.

3 Cut the second strip, using the right edge of the first strip as the cutting guide for the left edge of the second strip. Cut the right edge of the second strip in irregular waves.

4 Place the first strip in position over the foundation on the pinning board; pin. Cut the third strip, using the right edge of the second strip as the cutting guide for the left edge of the third strip and cutting the right edge as desired.

5 Cut each strip, using the previous strip as a cutting guide for the left edge. Pin each strip in position over the foundation after using it as a cutting guide. This will ensure the strips are placed in the correct order. When you reach the outer corner of the foundation, repeat the process in the other direction to cover the other half of the foundation.

6 Cut a second set of strips to weave perpendicular to the first set, following the same process. Weave the second set of strips through the first set, aligning the edges snugly while keeping the strips flat. Pin them in position.

7 Cover the woven pieces with a press cloth; press lightly to partially fuse the interfacing to the woven piece. Remove the woven piece from the pinning board and place it facedown on a pressing surface. Press again to completely fuse the interfacing.

8 Stitch over the raw edges of every strip in both directions, using a multistitch zigzag. Cut a 17" (43 cm) square and a 5" (12.7 cm) square from the woven piece.

9 Cut 6" × 18" (16 × 46 cm) rectangles from two of the solid wools and matching pieces of batting and backing fabrics, and quilt the blocks as desired. Trim the blocks to 5" × 17" (12.7 × 43 cm). Or cut two plain 5" × 17" (12.7 × 43 cm) rectangles.

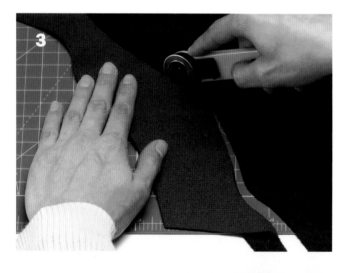

10 Stitch one solid rectangle to one side of the large woven square, using 1/2" (1.3 cm) seam allowances. Press the seam allowances open. Stitch a short end of the other solid rectangle to the small woven square; press seam allowances open. Then stitch the two pieces together, aligning the seam intersections.

11 Stitch a decorative trim over the center of the velvet ribbon. Center the ribbon over one seam of the pillow, and stitch down the outer edge to secure. Stitch the other decorative trim over the remaining long seam.

12 Prepare the pillow back and stitch it to the front, following the directions for a knife-edge pillow (page 10). Handstitch tassels at the pillow corners. Insert the pillow form.

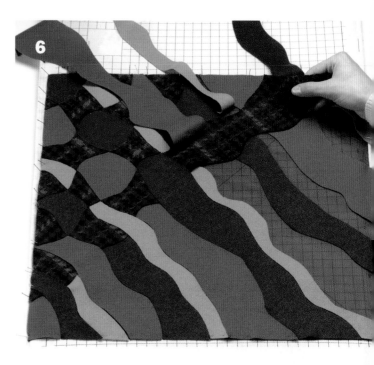

Mitered Stripes

Striped fabrics can easily be maneuvered to create dramatic patterns. With a little planning, triangles and bias-cut rectangles of striped fabric can be mitered together to form eye-catching diagonals, zigzags, or chevrons.

When you are shopping for the fabric, keep in mind that there are two basic types of stripes: regular and irregular. Regular stripes repeat the same pattern from both directions. Irregular stripes, like the ones in the pillows on the left, repeat in a one-way pattern. Both types can be mitered, but the irregular stripes may require more fabric. It would help to have your pattern pieces cut before you go to the store.

MATERIALS

Basic sewing supplies

Paper and tissue paper for making the pattern

Striped fabric, amount determined after drawing pattern

Thread to match fabric

Cording and coordinating solid fabric for making welting, or purchased welting

Welting foot or zipper foot

Zipper or fasteners for closure, as desired

16" (40.5 cm) square pillow form

CLOSURE SUGGESTIONS

Lapped back closure (plain or with fasteners)

Conventional zipper in pillow back

Mitered Stripes

TWO-TRIANGLE MITERED-STRIPE PILLOW

1 Draw a 16" (40.5 cm) square on a piece of paper; mark the top and bottom. Draw a diagonal seamline from corner to corner. Draw a continuous grain/stripe guideline parallel to and equal distance from adjoining sides, turning a 90-degree corner at the seamline. Cut out the square and cut it apart at the seamline. Trace the triangles onto tissue paper and add 1/2" (1.3 cm) seam allowances around each piece. Transfer the top and bottom markings and the exact placement of the grain/stripe guidelines.

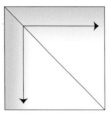 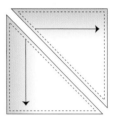

2 Spread the fabric on the cutting surface in a single layer. Arrange the pattern pieces on the fabric, aligning the guidelines of each triangle to the same location in the stripe sequence. The two straight edges that align to the lengthwise grain must align to the same stripe. Note that the edges marked top and bottom will be perpendicular to each other and the bias edges of the triangles angle in opposite diagonal directions. Pin in place, and cut out the pieces.

3 Pin the triangles, right sides together, along the bias edges, matching the stripes. Pin frequently to avoid shifting. Stitch the seam 1/2" (1.3 cm) from the edges. Check for accurate mitering of the stripes, and make adjustments, if necessary. Press the seam allowances open, taking care not to stretch the seams.

4 Prepare welting (page 30) and stitch it to the outer edge of the front. If the back will have a closure, follow the cutting directions for the closure style (page 22). Prepare the pillow back, and stitch it to the front to complete the pillow, following the directions for a knife-edge pillow (page 10).

FOUR-STRIP CHEVRON PILLOW

1 Draw a 16" (40.5 cm) square on a piece of paper. Draw three equally spaced vertical seams. Draw a continuous grain/stripe guideline that zigzags from the bottom line at 45-degree angles to the strip sides, turning a 90-degree corner at each seamline. It may be helpful to draw a second guideline at the opposite end. Number the strips from left to right. Cut out the square and cut it apart at the seamlines. Trace the strips onto tissue paper and add 1/2" (1.3 cm) seam allowances around each piece. Transfer the exact placement of the grain/stripe guidelines.

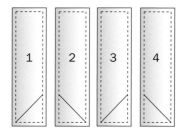 

2 Spread the fabric on the cutting surface in a single layer. Arrange the pattern pieces on the fabric, aligning the guidelines of each piece to the same location in the stripe sequence. Note that strips 1 and 3 will angle in the opposite diagonal direction of strips 2 and 4. Pin in place, and cut out the pieces.

3 Pin strips 1 and 2, right sides together, along the bias edges, matching the stripes. Pin frequently to avoid shifting. Stitch the seam 1/2" (1.3 cm) from the edges. Add strips 3 and 4. Check for accurate mitering of the stripes, and make adjustments, if necessary. Press the seam allowances open, taking care not to stretch the seams.

4 Finish the pillow as in step 4, opposite, but stitch the welting to the pillow back first because the pillow front edges are all on the bias and could stretch out of shape.

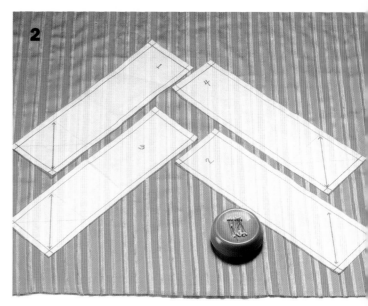

OTHER MITERING OPTIONS:

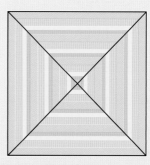

Four triangles with pillow sides cut on lengthwise grain

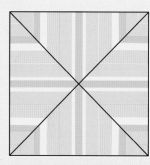

Four triangles with pillow sides cut on crosswise grain

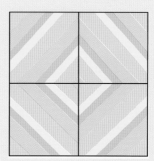

Four squares cut so stripes chevron outward

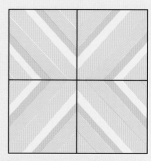

Four squares cut so stripes chevron inward

Silk Ties Reborn

Men's neckties are often made of gorgeous silk and silk-like fabrics. As fashions change, outdated ties end up in thrift shops or at the back of the closet. This tailored, hexagonal box pillow is a great way to use these wonderful fabrics.

The hexagonal design is created with a quilting technique known as foundation piecing. The seams that join the pieces also secure them to a muslin foundation that provides stability. Because neckties are cut on the bias, strips are easily cut for the welting along the length of the tie. Strips for piecing the pillow front and back are cut diagonally across the bottom of the ties on the straight grainline of the fabric.

You'll need seven ties to make this pillow. For the hexagon in the center, select a tie with a medium-size motif. Then select three ties in each of two coordinating colors with different patterns and designs. If you don't find the right combination of ties in a closet at home, just visit a thrift store to find limitless possibilities.

MATERIALS

Basic sewing supplies

Seven neckties

Seam ripper

Mesh laundry bag

Washing machine and detergent

³/8 yd (0.35 m) muslin or other lightweight cotton fabric

Rotary cutter, cutting mat, and heavy plastic ruler

Thread to match fabrics

Cording for welting

Zipper

Polyester fiberfill

CLOSURE SUGGESTIONS

Zipper in boxing strip

Silk Ties Reborn

1 Remove the stitches down the center backs of the ties, using a seam ripper. Remove any labels from the tie backs. Remove and discard the interfacing.

2 Place the ties in a mesh laundry bag and launder in cold water and mild detergent with minimal agitation. Lay them flat to dry. Press.

3 Trace and cut out the pattern for the hexagon center. Place the pattern in the center of a 12" (30.5 cm) muslin foundation square and, using a ruler, mark lines that extend from each side of the hexagon to the outer edge. Mark three more lines 1" (2.5 cm) apart and parallel to the first lines on each side of the hexagon.

4 Use the pattern to cut a central motif from the first tie fabric. Pin the center hexagon to the center of the foundation.

5 Cut 1½" (3.8 cm) strips on the straight grain from the wide bottom areas of the remaining ties. You will need two to four strips of each fabric. To be sure you save enough fabric for the boxing strip, cut the strips as you need them.

6 Cut three strips of the second fabric about 1" (2.5 cm) longer than one side of the center hexagon. Align the cut edge of one strip to the top edge of the center hexagon (side 1 on the pattern) and marked line on the foundation, right sides together. Stitch ¼" (6 mm) from the edges, stitching through both tie fabrics and the foundation; begin and end even with the lines of the adjoining sides. Stitch the remaining two strips to sides 3 and 5.

7 Press the strips away from the center. Trim off the ends even with the marked lines. Pin in place so the edges align to the next tier of marked lines.

Template shown at 100%

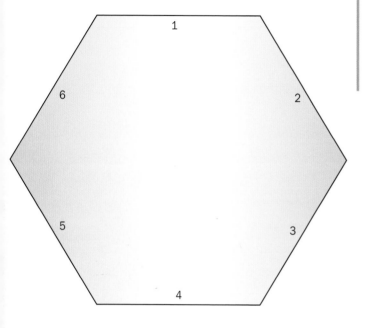

Diagram

3

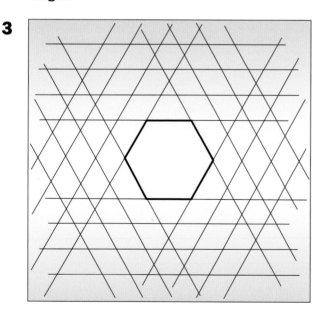

8 Cut three strips of the third fabric about 1" (2.5 cm) longer than an open side, including the width of the strips that have already been attached. Stitch the strips to the open sides (2, 4, and 6). Press away from the center, aligning the cut edges to the next tier of marked lines.

9 Repeat steps 6 to 8 using the fourth and fifth tie fabrics and adding them in the same sequence. Take care to stitch accurate 1/4" (6 mm) seams. Add the last tier of strips from the sixth and seventh fabrics to complete the pillow front. Stitch a scant 1/4" (6 mm) from the outer edges of the last tier of strips.

10 Make a pillow back to match the pillow front. Trim away the foundation fabrics along the outer edges of the last ring of strips.

11 Cut bias strips down the length of the desired tie fabrics; make and apply welting to the outer edges of the pillow front and back (page 30).

12 If you want a zipper opening in the boxing strip, cut two 2" (5 cm) strips from each of two fabrics for the zipper section of the boxing strip; cut them 1/2" (1.3 cm) longer than the length of one pillow side. Join the strips in sets of two with 1/2" (1.3 cm) seams; press the seams open. Then baste the sets together lengthwise with a 1/2" (1.3 cm) seam. Sew in a zipper (page 24).

13 Cut boxing strip pieces from the remaining tie fabrics 3" (7.5 cm) wide by the length of one side of the pillow. Join the pieces, together with the zipper section, into a ring. Apply the boxing strip to finish the pillow (page 17), positioning the seams at the corners of the pillow.

14 Stuff the pillow with polyester fiberfill.

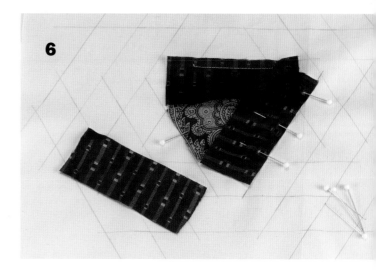

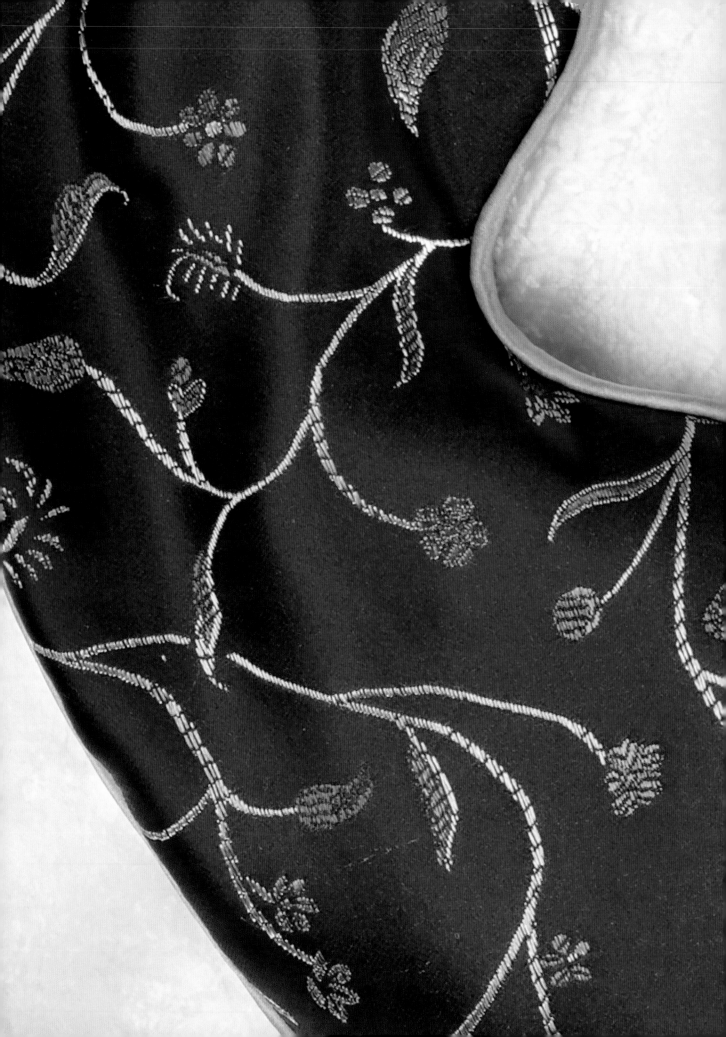

COMFORTING & COZY

The fundamental purpose of a pillow is to make life a little more comfortable, and the pillows in this group really deliver. Each is designed to soothe, cushion, cuddle, or coddle you in a special way. While designed for function, these pillows are also a delight to the senses, with beautiful fabrics and distinctive details. Indulge yourself with these pillows or give them to someone special.

Soothing Eye Bag

Rest your weary eyes under a cool, silky smooth pillow. This pillow is shaped to fit over the bridge of your nose and is filled with flaxseed to conform to your eyes and temples while adding just enough weight to press down gently. Before filling, the flaxseed can be scented with a couple drops of an essential oil, such as rosemary, lavender, or eucalyptus, if you find the aroma soothing. Keep the pillow in the freezer in a plastic bag so it will be chilled and ready whenever you need it. If you practice yoga or meditate, you can also use the eye bag during relaxation.

The narrow piping along the edge helps hold the pillow's shape while accenting the lovely silk print. The piping is made like the welting on page 30 but is filled with soft yarn instead of cording.

MATERIALS

Basic sewing supplies
Tissue paper for tracing the pattern
1/4 yd. (0.25 m) silk brocade or similar fabric
1/4 yd. (0.25 m) coordinating silk charmeuse or similar fabric
Thread to match fabric
1 1/2 yd. (1.4 m) yarn (any color)
Tapestry needle (blunt point)
1 cup flaxseed
Essential oil, optional

Soothing Eye Bag

1 Enlarge the pattern and trace it onto tissue paper; cut it out. Use the pattern to cut a pillow front from silk brocade and a pillow back from silk charmeuse. Also cut bias strips 1³/₈" (3.5 cm) wide from the charmeuse and piece them together, as necessary, to make a length of about 25" (63.5 cm).

2 Fold the bias strip in half, wrong sides together. Stitch ½" (1.3 cm) from the edges, taking care not to distort the width of the strip.

3 Thread yarn through a tapestry needle so you have two tails of equal length. Insert the needle into the piping tunnel and feed the yarn all the way through. Cut off the needle.

4 Pin the piping to the pillow front, aligning the raw edges. Overlap the ends below one eye, allowing them to trail off the raw edge. Clip the piping flange along the curves, as necessary, to allow the piping to lay flat. Machine-baste on the stitching line.

5 Pin the pillow front and back, right sides together. Stitch from the wrong side of the pillow front, just inside the basting line and crowding the piping. Leave a 3" (7.5 cm) opening along the top.

6 Clip the seam allowances of the pillow front, back, and piping flange around the nose curve. Turn back and press the seam allowances at the opening. Trim the rest of the seam allowances to ¼" (6 mm).

7 Turn the pillow right side out. Fill the pillow through the opening with flaxseed (scented with essential oil, if desired). Slipstitch the opening closed, taking small stitches.

3

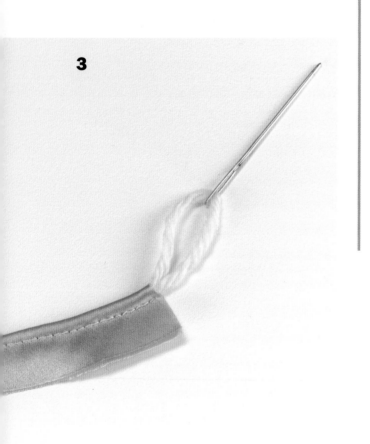

6

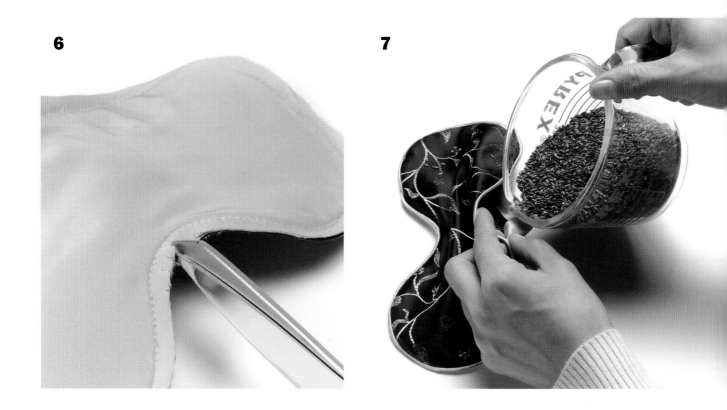

7

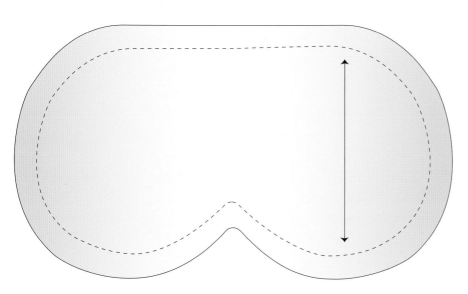

Pattern shown at 50%

Hot or Cold Shoulder Wrap

After one of those days when stress has locked your shoulders in knots, come home to a soothing shoulder wrap. This unique pillow has curved channels filled with rice; heat the inner pillow in the microwave or chill it in the freezer for added comfort. The weight of the rice coaxes your shoulder muscles to relax, and the clever design keeps the wrap in place even if you move around. The removable, washable cover has a taffeta side to give you calming coolness and a velveteen side for gentle warmth.

Sheila Duffy, who made many of the pillows in this book, combined her expert sewing skills and pattern-drafting ability to engineer our ideas into this ingenious pillow.

MATERIALS

Basic sewing supplies

Copy machine

5/8 yd. (0.6 m) cotton muslin or broadcloth for inner pillow

Tracing paper and tracing wheel

Thread to match fabrics

Pastry bag

3 lbs. (1.3 kg) rice

5/8 yd. (0.6 m) washable taffeta for outer cover

5/8 yd. (0.6 m) washable velveteen for outer cover

1/4 yd. (0.5 m) hook and loop tape

Hot or Cold Shoulder Wrap

1 Enlarge the pattern on pages 148 and 149, using a copy machine, and cut it out. Cut out two inner pillow pieces from muslin. Using tracing paper and a tracing wheel, transfer the stitching lines for the channels and shoulders to the right side of one piece.

2 Press under ½" (1.3 cm) seam allowances at the narrow ends of each piece. Pin the pieces right sides together. Stitch ½" (1.3 cm) seam on the inner and outer curves, leaving the ends open. Clip the neck edge curve to within ⅛" (3 mm) of the stitching line.

3 Turn the inner pillow right side out. Press. Stitch the channels and one shoulder line.

4 Place the tip of a pastry bag into the outer channel on the side with the open shoulder. Pour rice into the bag, filling the channel to within 2" (5 cm) of the open shoulder line. Repeat for each channel.

5 Pin across the channels to keep the rice back from the shoulder line. Stitch across the shoulder line. Remove the pins.

Tip: *Take care not to stitch over rice grains as they are hard enough to break the sewing machine needle.*

6 Fill the front channels of one side, one at a time to within 1" (2.5 cm) of the open ends. Pin across the channels to keep the rice back from the openings. Edgestitch the end closed. Repeat for the other side.

7 Cut one velveteen piece and one taffeta piece for the pillow cover. Turn under and stitch ½" (1.3 cm) double-fold hems on the narrow ends.

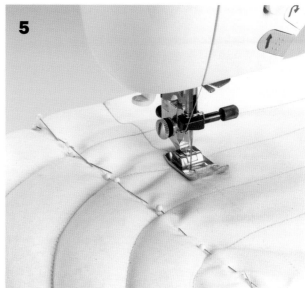

8 Cut two 4½" (11.5 cm) strips of hook and loop tape. Cut the strips in half lengthwise. Stitch the hook strips to the inside hems of the taffeta piece; stitch the loop strips to the inside hems of the velveteen piece.

9 Place the pieces right sides together. Stitch ½" (1.3 cm) seam on the inner and outer curves, leaving the ends open. Clip the neck edge curve to within ⅛" (3 mm) of the stitching line. Finish the seam allowances together. Turn right side out.

10 Slip the inner pillow into the cover. Join the hook and loop tapes to close the ends.

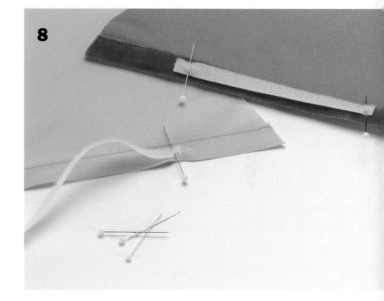

Pattern shown at 50%

**Enlarge both patterns to 100% then match
A to A and B to B. Tape together.**

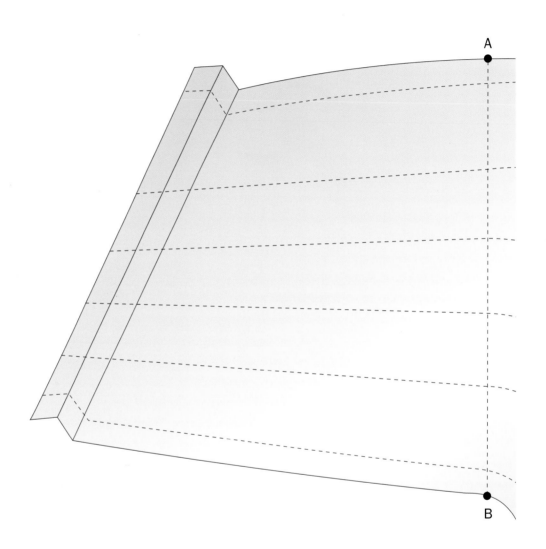

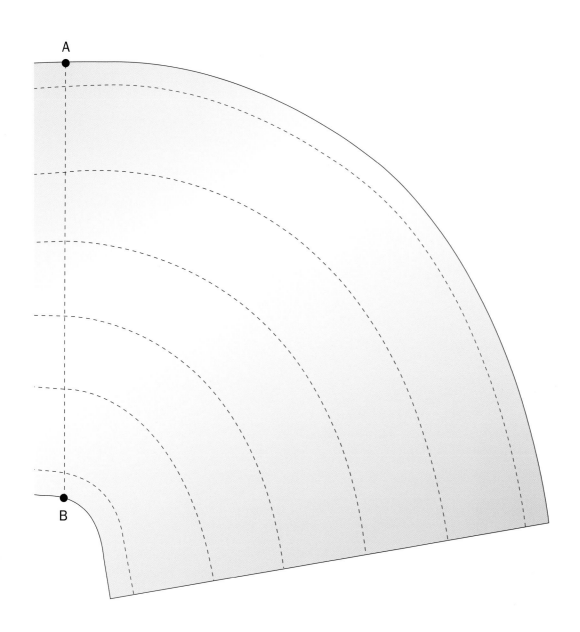

Convertipillow

This cozy fleece pillow is actually a convenient package that unfolds into a generous blanket with a pocket that holds a flannel pillow. Take one to a football or hockey game. Keep one in the car for napping on long trips. Make a couple for the kids to stretch out in front of the television. Send one to preschool for naptime. Everybody needs a convertipillow. Fleece is easy to sew and totally washable, so don't be afraid to give your convertipillow a workout.

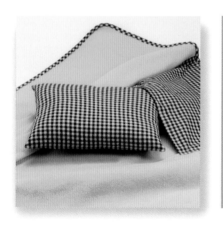

MATERIALS

Basic sewing supplies

1³/4 yd. (1.6 m) polyester fleece, 60" (152.5 cm) wide

Saucer

1¹/2 yd. (1.4 m) flannel

9" (23 cm) invisible zipper for inner pillow

12" × 16" (30.5 × 40.5 cm) pillow form

Two plastic side-release buckles

Fabric gluestick, optional

Convertipillow

1 Cut a fleece rectangle 63" × 52" (160 × 132 cm). Round the corners, using a saucer as a guide. Cut enough 2" (5 cm) bias strips of flannel to seam together to a length of 260" (660 cm). Cut two 13" × 17" (33 × 43 cm) rectangles of flannel for the pillow front and back. Cut a 16" × 20" (40.5 × 51 cm) rectangle of flannel for the pillow pocket. Cut two 2½" × 34" (6.5 × 86.5 cm) strips of flannel for the straps.

2 Make a knife-edge flannel pillow (page 10), inserting an invisible zipper (page 25).

3 Press under 1" (2.5 cm) twice on one long edge of the pocket piece. Edgestitch along the inner fold, forming a hem. Press under ½" (1.3 cm) on the short sides.

4 Center the pillow pocket, right side up, along one narrow edge of the wrong side of the blanket, with the hemmed edge inward. Baste ¼" (6 mm) from the raw edges. Edgestitch along the sides of the pocket. Stitch again ⅜" (1 cm) away from the edges; stitch an X to reinforce the inner corners.

5 Stitch the bias strips together, using ¼" (6 mm) seams; press seam allowances open. Press under one long edge ⅜" (1 cm); press under ⅜" (1 cm) on the diagonal end where stitching will begin.

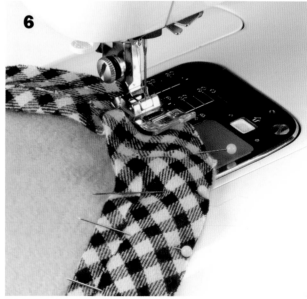

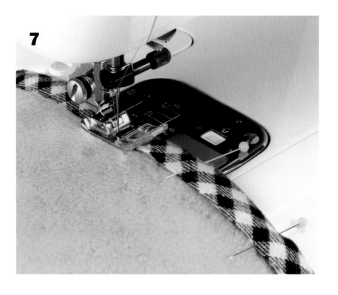

7

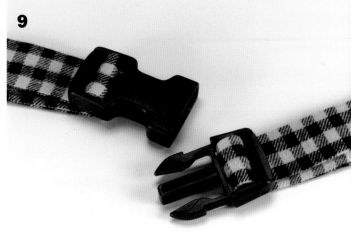

9

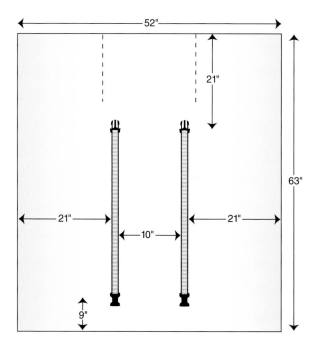

6 Stitch the right side of the bias strip to the blanket back, matching the raw edges and stitching 3/8" (1 cm) from the edges. Begin on one long side. Ease the strip around the corners. Keep the bias strip slightly taut on the stretchy top and bottom of the blanket to avoid ripples. Overlap the ends 1/2" (1.3 cm); trim excess diagonally.

7 Turn the bias to the front. Align the pressed fold to the previous stitching line, encasing the raw edges of the pillow pocket; pin or secure with gluestick. Topstitch close to the fold.

8 Fold the straps in half lengthwise, right sides together. Stitch 1/4" (6 mm) seam on the long edge. Turn right side out and press.

9 Insert one strap end through a buckle part; turn the fabric under 2" (5 cm), and stitch to secure. Repeat at the opposite end with the other buckle part. Repeat for the other strap and buckle.

10 Spread out the blanket, pocket side down. Pin the straps in place, following the diagram. Edgestitch down both sides and across the stitching lines of each strap.

11 Insert the pillow into the pocket. Fold the blanket sides completely over the pillow. Turn the pillow down twice. Turn the blanket bottom up to meet the pillow. Then fold the blanket up once again and secure the buckles.

Lumbar Luxury

When you sit in a chair with your feet flat on the floor, your lower back should rest against the chair back. Unfortunately, many chairs and sofas don't fit many people. Deep cushions and pillowy backs on a sofa or overstuffed chair may look cozy and comfortable, but they can be a real pain in the back if they cause you to slump into an unnatural, unsupported curve. A small, rectangular pillow placed at the back of a chair or sofa cushion can provide comforting support for the lower back, the part called the lumbar. It can also be helpful while driving.

As this designer lumbar pillow shows, back support doesn't have to look therapeutic. A luxurious tapestry fabric and rich cotton chenille brush fringe make this knife-edge pillow an attractive accent piece for a sofa or chair. It is stuffed with a standard pillow form that will conform to your back but bounce back to shape when you get up. To make the most of the nondirectional geometric design, the pillow was made from one piece of fabric, cut on the crosswise grain, with seams only at the bottom and sides. Because the pillow is intended to sit upright at the back of a sofa or chair, the fringe is only in the side seams.

1 Cut a rectangle of fabric 16" × 24" (40.5 × 61 cm). Mark the centers of the long sides.

2 Cut two 15½" (39.3 cm) lengths of fringe. Secure them to the long edges, as on page 34, from the center marks to ½" (1.3 cm) from the ends.

3 Fold the pillow cover in half, right sides together, encasing the fringe. Insert an invisible zipper in the bottom seam (page 25). Finish sewing the pillow sides.

4 Turn the pillow cover right side out and insert the form.

MATERIALS

Basic sewing supplies
½ yd. (0.5 m) tapestry fabric
¾ yd. (0.7 m) brush fringe
Thread to match fabric
12" (30.5 cm) invisible zipper
12" × 16" (30.5 × 40.5 cm) pillow form

CLOSURE SUGGESTION

Invisible zipper in bottom seam

Faux Fur Lounger

Oversized floor pillows are for lounging in front of the fireplace, playing board games, or watching television. They can also provide additional seating for large informal gatherings. Kids and teens love them! If you choose the fabric wisely, your pillow can be comfortable and stylish but practical, too. This realistic jaguar print fabric is a durable, furry, synthetic knit that is stable (it doesn't stretch) and machine washable. The pillow cover was made following the directions for a mock box pillow (page 12) but the corners were shaped before the outer seam was sewn, so the corded welting is not interrupted at the corners. The welting is more than an attractive accent. It makes the seam stronger so it can stand up to the wear and tear of everyday use.

1 Cut a 30" (76 cm) square for the pillow front. Prepare a 30" (76 cm) back, following the directions for inserting a conventional zipper (page 24) near one side.

2 Fold the front in half diagonally. At a corner, mark a line perpendicular to the cut edges 3" (7.5 cm) from the corner. Stitch. Trim off the corner triangle 1/2" (1.3 cm) from the stitching, press the seam allowances open. Repeat at each corner of the front and back.

3 Prepare welting (page 30). Attach the welting to the edge of the pillow front. Stitch the front to the back, right sides together. Turn right side out through the zipper opening.

4 Prepare the corners of the pillow form, following steps 3 and 4 for the mock box pillow (page 13), but working from the outside of the form. Insert the form into the pillow cover.

MATERIALS

Basic sewing supplies

1²/₃ yd. (1.58 m) animal print stable knit fabric, 60" (152.5 cm) wide (twice as much will be needed if fabric is narrower or if it is necessary to match the print).

Thread to match fabric

18" (46 cm) conventional zipper

Coordinating fabric and cording for making welting, or 4 yd. (3.7 m) ready-to-use welting

30" (76 cm) square pillow form

CLOSURE SUGGESTION

Conventional zipper near one side

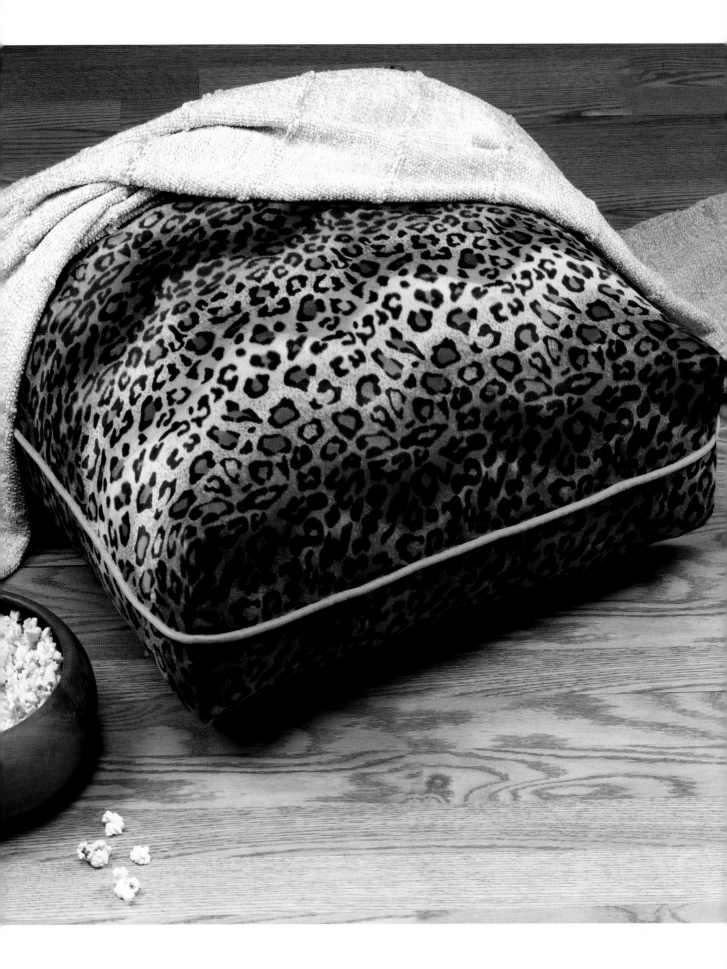

Sources

Dharma Trading Company
P.O. Box 150916
San Raphael, CA 94915
800-542-5227
email: catalog@dharmatrading.com
www.dharmatrading.com
(dyes, paints, fabrics, and
supplies for coloring fabric)

G Street Fabrics
www.gstfabrics.com
(quilting stencils, fabrics)

Jones Tones
33865 United Avenue
Pueblo, CO 81001
719-948-0048
www.jonestones.com
(foiling products)

Moondance Color Company
622 Spencer Road
Oakham, MA 01068
508-882-3383
www.moondancecolor.com
(felted wool, rug hooking
fabrics and supplies)

Rupert, Gibbon & Spider, Inc.
P.O. Box 425
Healdsburg, CA 95448
800-442-0455
www.jacquardproducts.com
(dyes, paints, fabric)

Screen Trans Development Corp.
100 Grand Street
Moonachie, NJ 07074
201-933-7800
(foiling products)

Tandy Leather Company
P.O. Box 791
Fort Worth, TX, 76101
800-433-3201 Ext. 1317
www.tandyleather.com

Thai Silks
252 State Street
Los Altos, CA 94022
800-221-7455
www.thaisilks.com
(silk fabrics)

Index

$\mathcal{I}$ndex